How to
Date
Your Wife

How to Date Your Wife

STAN CRONIN

Second Printing: July 2004

**International Standard Book Number
0-88290-761-1**

**Horizon Publishers' Catalog and Order Number
C2103**

Printed and distributed
in the United States of America by

Mailing Address:
925 North Main
Springville, Utah 84663

Phone and Fax:
Local Phone: (801) 489-4084
Toll Free: 1 (800) SKYBOOK
FAX: (801) 489-1097

www.cedarfort.com

Contents

Contents   7

Dedication

To the most important person in my life,

my wife, Jereyne

Her work ethic and discipline to do daily what is necessary have truly made her my helpmeet. Her courage to face each day with a smile inspires me. Her acceptance of responsibility as a mother and wife is my guiding star and has encouraged me to be a better husband and father. Her honesty, faith and loyalty are uplifting; her compassion and friendship unmatched. She has been my confidante in strife and my partner in creating life. I truly love her!

Acknowledgments

I must thank my parents, Stanley D. Cronin, Sr. and Jewell Cronin. They were the first married couple I observed dating. In this they taught me well. I love them for all they have done for me; I only hope I can repay that debt someday.

My in-laws, Al and Geneyne Clark, have been an inspiring example of what a dating couple should be like. They have shown that dating does take place in the middle-aged years and beyond and that time does not dull the need for togetherness. I thank Geneyne for lovingly bearing and rearing the child who grew into the fine young lady I married thirty years ago.

My deepest thanks to my wife, Jereyne, for supporting me in this project as she has in every endeavor I have attempted. Her belief in me and her support have provided the foundation I needed to make this book a reality. In this, as in everything I do, she has helped make me what I am.

I appreciate my children, Jacey, Jared, and Jenny, for allowing me the time necessary to complete this book. Along with my wife, they helped pass out questionnaires in Arizona while temperatures soared over 100 degrees. They have been a joy in my life. I wish for them as much happiness as life can give.

Judi Villa of the Arizona Republic newspaper gave me a boost when she decided to do an article on the book before it was written. Her article spawned inquiries from local and national television shows, which caused me to quicken my pace in finishing the book. Thanks for the article and the push, Judi.

Dr. Dennis R. Deaton influenced my life by teaching me how to manage my life and my thoughts. I learned from him that all things are possible when I act instead of being acted upon. His insights are helping me achieve my dreams.

Thanks to Collette Lewis and Cecily Markland for their excellent editing skills. Don Evans, Allison Drew, Cheryl Cooning and Randi Knappenberger read and made relevant suggestions to improve the manuscript at various stages.

I wish I could thank men such as Abraham Lincoln, Aristotle, Shakespeare, Benjamin Franklin and dozens of others whose wisdom has outlived them. Their ideas, thoughts, letters, stories and poems appear in this work. Their words still speak plainly to us. Truth will always be truth, no matter how much a man may fight it.

More than anyone can know, I am appreciative of the wives who took the time to fill out and return my questionnaire. Without their thoughts and help, this book would never have been possible. Every survey returned aided in my search for what I needed to know. I learned from each survey, particularly from the one filled out by my own wife. Thank you all for your generous sharing. I hope your husbands will carry out some suggestions compiled in this book and you will reap the happiness you want and deserve.

Introduction

Read not to contradict and confute; nor to believe and take for granted; nor to find talk and discourse; but to weigh and consider. Some books are to be tasted, others to be swallowed, and some few to be chewed and digested. . . . Reading maketh a full man.

—*Francis Bacon*

This book is for weighing and considering. It is for chewing and tasting. It will make you full. If you never planned to read a book like this, we're even. I had no idea I would write it and the only reason you have it in your hands is that I care and so do you. My normal work is neither artistic nor romantic. I am a retired police officer of the Phoenix Police Department. As a twenty-year veteran, what I have seen is truly different from love letters and candlelight dinners. I have seen the deterioration of the family and the corruption of marriage vows played out in vivid, blood-and-guts living color.

Though it had nothing to do with dating and romance, what I saw was the foundation for this book. I started looking for answers, for ways I could avoid what was happening all around me. Wanting to discover how I could create a haven to go home to, a shelter from all that I saw at work, I started asking questions.

My research began in 1974 when I married Jereyne, although I did not know at the time that I was researching. As years passed, I became comfortable in my marriage. I had my space, my wife had hers and we shared time together. As additional years passed, my space became larger and her space became larger. The spaces that overlapped grew smaller.

This space problem grew with having children, building careers, pursuing outside interests and hobbies, taking college classes and completing church and community responsibilities'. We filled our time with a myriad of distractions. As our time together shrank, our spotlight on each other became less focused.

We changed all of that by beginning to date. When I got the idea to write this book, I knew my experiences with my own wife were not enough to provide answers for others. The quickest way to an answer is through a question. So I asked the experts: the wives themselves. Holding personal interviews with wives, some who live in my own neighborhood, I learned many new things. In addition, I created a questionnaire to gather ideas and responses from wives across the United States. I distributed one thousand questionnaires to married women in Arizona, Texas, Oklahoma, Arkansas, Tennessee, Kentucky, Missouri, Illinois, Washington, and Alaska.

Recorded between the covers of this book are the thoughts and reflections gathered from the completed questionnaires and personal interviews. The responses to the questionnaires were heartfelt, honest and in-depth. In essence, the thousands of responses boiled down to this: wives love their husbands. They want to be happy and they want their husbands to be happy.

A patrol car was my "on duty home" for nineteen of my twenty and a half years on the police department while I traveled from call to call. I saw the examples that fathers and mothers set in their homes. The reaction of the children to those examples has not been a positive one.

I have put fathers in jail for beating their wives. I heard the fear in their children's voices as I took "daddy" away. Many of those children were teenagers at the time. Within five years these teenagers were over twenty and I was putting them in jail for hitting their wives.

Within another ten to fifteen years, those former teenagers had children that were teenagers. The reactions of these teenagers to their girlfriends were the same as their parents' examples. I retired when I started putting the grandchildren in jail for beating their wives.

If you have children in your home, you need to be a role model to other husbands around you. Put your wife on a pedestal and see how she responds. You can make a difference.

I am a strong believer in cause and effect. There is a cause for most problems in the world. Parents cause broken homes by acting incorrectly in front of children. Broken homes cause juvenile delinquents who commit crime. Crime results in victims, which causes heartache for the victim, his family and friends. Then, there is the misery the criminal and his family must endure while he is in jail. The cost in tax dollars to house criminals is on our backs, causing us distress.

You can stop this cycle. It takes a commitment to start in your home. Do not worry about what is happening in other homes for now; just make it happen in your home. If you will treat your wife right by dating and showing your children you care for her, you can pass along a rich legacy for many generations to come.

A universal truth expressed by many wives is that they want to be cherished by their husbands. Being a man, and having many male friends who are husbands, I know that husbands want to be admired by their wives. Two totally different philosophies are involved.

While investigating these two philosophies, I found two more that involve the family. First, some families have a selfish, closed attitude, i.e., we are family so I can harm my family members physically or emotionally and treat them any way I want. The internal attitude of this kind of family is that what goes on in my family is nobody else's business. The second family philosophy was this: We are family so we respect one another, we love one another and we stick up for and protect each other from those outside the family. When I see to it that my wife's married years are her best, and when she gives her best years to me, this creates the happy marriage.

You will find hundreds of ideas in this book to help you contribute to your wife's happiness. You will find scores of dating ideas suggested by wives. You will find dozens of ways to be more successful as a husband.

If you want a good wife, it is up to you to make her so. If you are considerate of her, she will be conscious of you and your needs. Strengthen your marriage by focusing on what you can do, not on what she can or "should" do. As you apply the ideas in this book, she will become a better wife. In turn, you will become a better couple. To women who are reading this book, it is also true that you can greatly influence the kind of husband he is.

You see, men and women, for all our differences, have some basic similarities. I am a man who cares about his wife and my wife cares about me. We love each other and want the best for each other. I know that you also want the best for your spouse.

Agreeing with each other or talking when you do not agree is essential to a good marriage. You will come to understand each other and communicate better as you spend more time together. When you can understand one another, you will come to agree more often. It all hinges on spending time together.

Although this book is written to married men, I am not speaking solely to them. If you are a woman, married or single, or if you are a single man, apply the principles in this book. Although I address husbands throughout this book, a wife should read it not to find out what her husband should do, but what she can do. For those of you not yet married, do not read this to discover what you can do someday after you are married. Instead, look for things that you can do today to strengthen relationships, create love, and enjoy life to the fullest.

This book is to be a guide, first to increase your awareness of your dating habits. Second, it is a resource of ideas for improving your dating habits. As you begin to concentrate on her, you will be surprised how soon she starts considering your needs more often and more willingly.

If you are up for a challenge — this book is for you. The challenge is to read this book with an open mind and put into practice, patiently and with longsuffering, the ideas and suggestions listed within its pages. The reward for acting on these ideas is increased love and passion. When is the last time you actually used the word passion to describe your relationship with your wife? Institute just ten percent of the ideas in this book and passion can be yours again.

For those who feel there may be something in the book you might use, I promise you will find more in these pages than you could ever imagine. Take the chance that you may find a good quality between these covers. Take the chance that there may be some value here for you. There is.

If you are still doubtful, I suggest you put it to the test. Try it. Put into practice just one or two of the ideas this book suggests. You have everything to gain, especially your wife and her admiration for you.

Dating Defined

"If you'll toast the bagels and pour the orange juice, sweet-heart," said the newlywed bride, "breakfast will be finished."

"Good. What are we having for breakfast?" asked the new husband.

"Bagels and orange juice," the bride replied.

My wife and I have had a few breakfasts like that. Sometimes I made them and sometimes she did. These were dates.

What Is a Date?

In the world today, we use the word *date* almost daily. "What is today's date?" "Do you know the date of the negotiation meeting?" "Can we plan a date for the office party?" For the purposes of this book, the word *date* means an appointment for a husband and wife to spend a particular time with each other.

Occasionally, you will want to make a fairly formal *appointment* with your wife. Just as you schedule business appointments or vacations, some of your appointments with your wife should be planned days or weeks in advance. Pre-planning goes a long way when you are trying to show your wife you care about her. Both of you will enjoy having an appointed time to look forward to spending together.

However, you do not need a formal appointment to count time spent with your wife as a *date*. My wife and I have had dates that bloomed from spontaneous invitations, such as, "Want to grab a bite to eat?" or, "do you want to go shopping with me?" I surveyed many wives suggested they enjoy these types of spontaneous *dates*.

Any date requires spending time together. This time can be two seconds ("Come here, gorgeous, and let me kiss you"); two minutes (a song comes on the radio, you go into the kitchen, take your wife in your arms and dance with her); two hours (you go to a movie or to dinner together); two days (go to a motel for the weekend); two weeks (you take a trip to Hawaii for your twentieth anniversary); two lifetimes, (yours and hers).

An appointment to spend a particular time with . . .

Note that our definition does not say "by," or "in front of," or "at the same event as" another person. It says "with."

A Date Requires Interaction

A date is time you spend together, participating in activities that help you relate to each other in some way. A date requires interaction. Do not merely attend a movie or athletic event together—interact! Speak to her about the event, hold her hand, and glance over at her from time to time. In other words, share the time together.

A Woman Needs "Listening to" and "Talking with"

One wife wrote, "Many men subconsciously think that being present physically means 'I love you, because I am with you.' A woman needs listening to and talking with to feel loved."

Imagine for a moment a vacuum cleaner salesman arriving on a sales call. He looks great with his hair combed, shoes polished and clothes clean. He is smiling. He hustles and is determined to make the sale. If you're not home, he calls back. What if you put that kind of effort into dating your wife?

You will see a phrase repeated throughout this book. "There is no substitute for spending time with your wife." This is the crux of the book. If it will get you to spend a little more time with the woman you married, then it will have done what it was intended to do. Your happiness and joy will increase as you spend more time together. Passion awaits you.

Don't Compare Your Marriage to Others

This book should not create confrontation. There will be conflict if you try to compare your marriage to any other marriage. There will be conflict if either one of you tries to use this book to say, "Look at the things you could have done." Nobody wins in such a power struggle. Instead, create an atmosphere of thoughtfulness in your marriage. Speak softly and quietly to your wife about this book. Gordon B. Hinckley has said,

Quiet talk is the language of love. It is the language of peace. It is the language of God. It is when we raise our voices that tiny molehills of difference become mountains of conflict . . . Cultivate the art of the soft answer. It will bless your homes, it will bless your lives, it will bless your companionships, it will bless your children.

How to Start? Have Your Wife
Fill Out the Questionnaire

A dating questionnaire is in the back of the book. I suggest you make some copies. Have your wife fill it out. By the way, having your wife fill out the questionnaire and then discussing it (over dinner) would make an excellent date. Once she has filled it out, don't be disappointed if you do not score well in her answers. You need to know where you are so you can see where you need to go. Build on this starting point.

Next, begin putting into practice the suggestions in this book. Have your wife fill out the questionnaire again in six months so you can check your progress. After that, use the questionnaire once a year for a good measuring stick.

Today's the Perfect Date!

The word *date* also means a day of the month. Today — right now — is the perfect date to begin dating your wife. You cannot possibly use everything in this book the first month, or even the first year or two. Do try at least one idea today. Take your wife on a date on this very date.

2

Why You Should Read This Book

Do not consider painful what is good for you.
—Euripides

Most of us avoid pain, even when it is good for us. You may have received this book as a gift from your wife. It is even possible you are being coerced, bribed or otherwise enticed by a friend, consultant or marriage counselor to read it. Then again, you may be reading it because you have a genuine desire to find ways to return to the good times and put some fun back in your marriage.

Males seem to have some interesting traits in common. For example, at the outset of any endeavor, almost universally, men want to know, "What's in it for me?"

Why read this book? Why even consider dating your wife? If your relationship is already doing well, frequent, fun dating can keep your marriage from deteriorating and falling apart. Dating your wife can bolster a faltering marriage, too. It can fan the fires of love lying neglected inside the two of you.

The Valentine's Day Note and Rose

An illustration of what I am talking about is represented in this story of a friend. He knew I was writing this book, and

Valentine's Day was approaching. He asked me if I had any tips for him. I was glad he asked.

I suggested he stop by a florist on his way home and purchase a single red rose. (He didn't have money for a dozen.) Next, I told him to write a note to his wife telling her how much being his wife and the mother of his children meant to him, and I suggested that the note be between one half to one full page, handwritten. When he arrived home, he was to make the bed if it had not been made already. Then I advised him to leave the note on her pillow and put the rose on top of the note.

The next day he sought me out at work. He was smiling. He said, "Stan, I am not going to tell you what happened last night, but it was GREAT! It was one of the best Valentine's nights we have ever had." Small things lead to passion when you take a moment to think and then act.

If the weather is cold and frigid in your marriage, dating is something you can do to change it. In this era of divorce mania, doing something to shore up your marriage is reason enough to read this book. However, let me suggest that the rewards of dating your wife are much more specific and far more extensive than a mere marriage bandage. I can assure you that you will reap much more than you can now even imagine.

By dating your wife you will gain more of whatever it is you want out of life. Whatever now motivates you, you will stop merely pursuing and start obtaining. That is a huge promise, but I'm going to say it again. As odd as it may seem, you will obtain whatever it is you want most by applying even a little of what this book suggests. I must add if more sex is your only goal, you will not be sincere in your quest for a better marriage, and that insincerity will be very transparent.

Your Primary Goal: Make Your Wife Happy!

Your primary reason for practicing the ideas in this book must be to make your wife happy. By dating your wife and making her happy, you'll find love, appreciation and sex occurring naturally in your marriage. If you try to manipulate your wife for self-gratification, you will not fool her for long and you will lose her respect.

Perhaps money is the driving force behind your actions. By spending money to date your wife, you will be saving money in the end. Divorce is expensive. Statistics show "happily" married men are more successful in the work place. Translation: Happily married men make more money. It literally pays to date your wife.

Dating your wife pays in other ways as well. Payments that cannot even be quantified can be yours. How do you measure what it would be like to be greeted by a smiling wife when you get home from work? To have your wife be your confidante, your best friend, your partner? To have such a strong relationship with your wife that others envy you and come to you for advice? To feel confident that you are completely loved and accepted by your wife? To know she looks forward to spending time with you?

These things are just the beginning, what you could call the pocket change. Truth is truth, no matter where it comes from. Proverbs 31:28 reads, "Her children rise up, and call her blessed; her husband also, and he praiseth her."

The Eight-Cow Wife

Perhaps you know the story of the young Polynesian man who searched throughout the islands for a wife. The going dowry price for a wife at that time was a fish or a few chickens. For an unusually beautiful or talented girl, the great gift of a cow was offered. The young man of our story chose a maiden who had been teased all her life as the ugliest girl in the village. But he could see her potential and offered her father the unheard sum of eight cows. When the girl realized her value in the eyes of her husband, she truly became an "eight-cow wife."

Symbolically, only you can make your wife worth eight cows. Others may not see the value in her like you do—it is up to you. Are you going to treat her like a one-fish woman or an eight-cow wife?

What does this book contain for you? It contains ideas for your happiness, joy, contentment, satisfaction and comfort—in short, PEACE. By following the easy guidelines contained in these pages, your dreams can come true and you will have much fun along the way. It all starts with dating your wife.

3

How to Begin the Change

A man told his friend one day, "I can't break my wife of the habit of staying up till three in the morning."

"What is she doing staying up till three in the morning?" asked the friend.

Answered the husband, "Waiting for me to come home."

Let's start with some basics. A wife has the right to know where her husband is at three in the morning. The ideas, activities and techniques I provide throughout this book are not just my own ideas. They come from women like your own wife. I encourage you to value and carefully consider their suggestions.

The Basic Assumption

Start with the assumption that you still love one another. (The surveys definitely bear this out, at least from the wives' points of view.) It may have been days, months, even years since love has been expressed. Some of you may feel as if there is not much love left, but I can assure you, the feelings you shared before you were married are still there. Recreate them. Strengthen them. Reignite the fire with the spark that remains deep inside you. Remember, there is no substitute for spending time with your wife.

A wife is a very complex being, and yet, on the other hand, she is uncomplicated. She has many wants, but few needs. Husbands are the same. Most husbands have the same wants, but they also have relatively few needs. The needs shared by most couples are the needs to be loved and to be appreciated.

You Need to Confirm and Validate Your Words with Action

To me, *appreciation* and *love* are action words. These two words demand that you act to make them valid, to make them real. Without action, love and appreciation are only feelings. Without action, your wife never knows of your love and appreciation for her.

When you feel love toward your wife, you need to tell her. That one action can improve your life. However, telling her is not the action required if you want her to experience love. When you say, "I love you," she usually cannot feel what you are feeling at that instant. But she has felt your love in the past, so she knows what you are describing. However, showing her gives her the opportunity to have that feeling for herself. It provides her with loving, caring experiences. If she is having those experiences, you both will have passion in your experiences together.

When you act, the person you love can see that you love her. Along with sight, other senses often come into play. For example, the smell of roses, the taste of chocolate, or the touch of a gentle hug seems to contribute to and strengthen the experience. Actions confirm and validate your words. Your wife can see that you are not just talking about a word or a feeling, but mean what you are saying.

Practice Showing Your Love

Your wife will know you mean what you say when you act on the emotion of love. When both of you practice showing each other your love instead of just talking about it, your love grows stronger. By combining loving actions with words of love, your wife will easily recognize the reason behind the action. So, express your love, but act. When you plunge into the trap of just saying the word "love" with no actions to back it up, love diminishes and eventually extinguishes itself.

To test this point, try this: When you finish this chapter, get up and go to the nearest place you can find flowers—any species of flower will do. Get them out of your garden, the grocery store down the street, or from a florist. A woman never tires of receiving flowers. Once you obtain the flowers, go to your wife and give them to her with a big kiss and, most importantly, a hug that lasts for as long as she wants to snuggle in your arms. Say nothing. Just let your action convey the message. Now kiss her again while still holding her around the waist. Make it a passionate kiss. Hug her again. Finish by telling her, "I love you." The rest of the scenario I leave up to you. Experience the joy and passion.

I remember talking to an acquaintance and hearing him tell of his aspirations and dreams. At the end of his description, I asked him why he had not already accomplished some of his goals.

He replied, "I'm waiting for my ship to come in." I then told him, "If your ship has not come in, you need to find out where it is and go get it."

Stop Waiting for Your Ship to Come In

Many of you are *waiting* for what you want instead of going after it. It's the same in your marriages. If you are waiting for something to change in your marriage so it will get better, recognize that waiting is not going to correct the problem. However, you have something as powerful as any Super Hero. You have the power of your mind. You can accomplish things that seem impossible, when you focus on your goal and move to make things happen.

Use the ideas in this book to generate new ideas. Use the suggestions to stimulate your own thought processes, to find solutions and to prepare a course of action that will carry you through your troubles. Stop waiting for your ship to come in.

Act—Don't Wait to Be Acted Upon

I hope your relationship with your wife is sailing on smooth waters and needs only steady steering to keep it on course. If you are facing stormy waters, take actions to stay on course. Act—don't wait to be acted upon.

Think about the actions you are taking (or failing to take). Are you waiting for love or are you going after it? Do you expect your wife to show love toward you before you show your love to her? Are you waiting for just the right mood to hit you to start doing something about your relationship with your wife? Wait no more. Take action to save or improve your marriage. Start dating your wife again. Start being romantic.

4

Why Date Your Wife?

To educate a man in mind and not in morals is to educate a menace to society.
—*Theodore Roosevelt*

Education comes in many ways. You can attend school. Life's experiences can teach you many things whether you have them yourself or see others having them. The surveys collected during the research stage of this book were collected from currently married women. I will define "currently married" as meaning successfully married. These are the women we want to educate us. They can tell us what makes their marriages successful.

Always Treat a Lady with Respect

Your wife was a lady when you married her and she is a lady now. She may or may not behave like a lady all the time, but she is a lady nonetheless. I know you love your wife. Since you are reading this book, I have to assume you want to keep her as your wife.

Surely you married her because you loved her. When you were dating before marriage, I'll bet you loved talking to her and listening to her. I'll also bet she loved listening to you and responding to your thoughts. She is still the same person, although a little older and a lot wiser now. In case you have not noticed, you are also older, and I hope you are also wiser.

Time has a way of decaying our thoughts. An acquaintance recently told me, "My wife isn't half the woman she used to be." I responded, "Neither are you half the man you used to be, so that makes you even and still a good match for each other." Often we forget that time has taken its toll on us just as much as others.

We have this image in our minds of what we think we look like. You have an image of yourself that may not be the same as others have of you. Few of us look as good as we "think" we do, and none of us look as good as we did ten, twenty, or thirty years ago.

Communication Is the Key to a Good Marriage

You should date your wife to "be with" her. There is no substitute for spending time with your wife. There is nothing else that encourages communication like being together for one or several hours. Communication is the chief cornerstone of any good marriage.

To illustrate this last point, I would like to tell you of something police have termed "the Stockholm syndrome." The "syndrome" was first seen in Stockholm, Sweden. Briefly, the incident happened like this; many details have been left out of the story since they are not relevant:

A man took some hostages at gunpoint while in a building. Police surrounded the building, which forced the criminal and his hostages to be together for many hours. When the hostages started talking to the suspect, he responded to them. As talking progressed, the hostages and suspect discovered they understood each other more. By the time it was all over, the captor and the captured were comrades and the hostages supported the villain. They identified with the suspect. The suspect could no longer think of hurting his victims, and they did not want to see him harmed.

What caused this transformation from enmity to companions? Communication. The hostages and suspect were not just talking for a few minutes, but had discussions that covered many hours. It sounds strange, but it is a fact of communication. Those with whom we communicate, we like. The more we talk with someone, the more we like him or her. Still more communication and love develops.

I am sure that sometime in the past, you spent time with someone you did not know or did not like. You were uneasy at first. After a time, you became comfortable with that person. Ultimately, you became friends.

Try spending as much time talking to your wife as this criminal did with his victims. If you do this, you will relate to your wife much better than you do now. After hours of conversing, you would not even dream of speaking harshly to your wife, and she would have soft words for you in times of hardship.

Given the choice between sitting and talking with my wife one on one, heart to heart, soul to soul or coming home each day to a newspaper, television, or yelling, I'll take the peace and quiet of conversation. I highly recommend it to you. Take fifteen minutes today to sit and talk with your wife. You will be surprised how much more connected you will be with her in thought, and how much more you will be able to focus on the future after a few sessions like this.

Try to Create Fond Memories

Another motivation to date your wife is to create fun memories. Memories are what carry us through the arduous times or cause us to quit when the going gets rugged. Fond memories cause us to stick it out; adverse memories cause us to quit. Memories are funny things. Sometimes when we get older, our memories play tricks on us. Something that was horrifying at the time, such as falling and breaking a bone, you will remember as a funny event later. When you later tell the story of how you broke that bone, it usually will have become a funny story.

Painful things in memories eventually become pleasant, such as a woman having a baby. Not long after a baby is born, its birth is remembered as a wonderful, joyous occasion. But the fact is, at the actual time of the birth, the mother could have been screaming at her husband and condemning him for causing this "problem."

We do have unpleasant memories. However, most memories of those we love somehow always come out pleasant, funny and wonderful. Create memories now with your wife and you will have more wonderful, funny and pleasant things to remember with her later. Dating is for creating memories that are going to come out in years to come as the most pleasant things we can remember.

Grow in Your Appreciation for Each Other

When a man takes his wife out to dinner, a movie, or a drive to see a sunset, his wife appreciates his effort. When you make an effort to be with your wife, she notices. She may not always tell you she appreciates what you do for her, but she does. She will remember. Dating is also for increasing the love and appreciation you have for one another.

Be Willing to Serve Each Other

Willingly serving others always causes a person to feel fantastic. Think of the little things you have done for others over the years and the warm glow it gave you. A few years ago, I had a great experience I will never forget. I knew of a homeless man who slept in a pickup truck, usually parked at the corner of a busy intersection in Phoenix, Arizona. Most people do not realize it, but Phoenix gets cold in the winter. We had a cold spell where the temperature plummeted into the twenties.

One day, while I was working as a patrol officer, the dispatcher sent me to a call at a fast food restaurant, which was across the street from the place where this homeless person usually lived in his truck. The restaurant wanted him out of their dining room because the man smelled terribly. I approached the man and my nose told me that I wanted nothing to eat the rest of that day due to the smell emanating from him. While telling him as politely as I could that he had to leave the restaurant, I could hardly take a breath due to the odor. This man probably had not bathed in many months. In reality, there are not many showers available to a person in his condition.

He complied with my request to leave. As he left the establishment, I could not help but notice how tattered his coat was. It had holes in it, and I could see his shirt through his jacket in several places. My heart ached to send him into the cold morning air while he was wearing that jacket, but at the time, there was nothing I could do. The radio dispatcher was holding other calls from citizens that needed my assistance.

That night I did not sleep well. I could not get out of my mind how cold that man must be. Knowing he was sleeping in that truck with a temperature below freezing made me uneasy. I, on the other hand, had a warm house and a king-size bed, and the indoor temperature was hovering around sixty-seven degrees.

My shift started the next morning at five o'clock. As I left the door of my home that morning, the wind was blowing a little and it cut right through me. The coat closet is by our front door, so I reached in and took out a favorite jacket and carried it to the car with me.

Our briefing seemed to last forever that day. After loading and gassing the squad car, I headed for the intersection where

I knew I would find the man. I didn't even tell the radio dispatcher I was ready for calls. This time, the callers would have to wait. Arriving at the intersection, I located the truck parked on the northeast corner as usual. When I walked up to the truck, I found the window down part way and the man lying on the seat inside, sleeping. He had on the old, tattered jacket from the day before. He had one side of a cardboard box pulled over him as a makeshift blanket.

It sent a chill through me just thinking about having to sleep in those conditions. I knocked on the window. Even after several attempts, I couldn't wake the man. I began thinking he may have died due to the cold. Suddenly, he stirred and became startled. His relationship with police officers had not been a pleasant one over the years.

When I was finally able to speak with him, he would not open the door for me. Finally, I held up my jacket to the four-inch gap at the top of the window. Telling the man that I did not need this coat, I then asked him if he wanted it. He jerked the jacket through the window so fast I thought he was going to pull my arm off before I could release my hold on it.

As he put on his new jacket, I walked away. He didn't have to tell me he appreciated that jacket. I knew he did. The rest of that day, I felt great. This small act brought me a fabulous feeling. There were no bad radio calls that day for me. I was walking on air.

So that you will not think too highly of me, I owned other jackets at the time and really could do without that one jacket. I have never missed it. The man and his truck were gone a few days later—he moved on to parts unknown and I never saw him again.

Now, what has this got to do with dating? You can rest assured that you can have many such good feelings when you do something for your wife. Making a date with your wife is an act of service. Her service to you comes in many forms. Most wives cook, clean, wash, iron, play taxi for kids, pick up your underwear, and tuck you in bed after making love to you. It is a small thing to give your wife some of your time for all that she does for you.

My survey shows women don't even care that much about money. We will talk about that in the chapter entitled, "Your Illusions about Dating." Some men have assumed that money was the number one thing on a woman's mind. Money is on the mind of a woman who is divorcing, but not to a woman who plans to stay married.

Give of Yourself

A woman who wants to stay married requires that you give of yourself and spend time with her. To her, the money is secondary and comparatively speaking, unimportant. A woman makes money more important and places it higher on her priority list only when she cannot have you and your time. She uses money to replace you. When she has you and your time, her need for money decreases.

Enjoy the "Ripple Effect"

Doing good things for your wife usually has a ripple effect. Tossing a stone in a pool of water causes ripples to surge in every direction from the center point. Doing good things for your wife will cause her to reciprocate good to you and to others. There is nothing that will give you more happiness than serving your wife. What goes around comes around.

One day when I was close to finishing this book, I was watching the noon news. They announced a newly completed study by the United Nations. The study concluded, "Women are overworked, underpaid and under-appreciated." It also said that women do 53 percent of the work in the world.

Now, how in the world (pun intended) did they figure that out? Regardless, let's assume the study has some validity. All men have to do to be equal in work is three percent more. That would give both sides a balance of joy. The part of the study of interest to me was the part that says women are "overworked and under-appreciated." You cannot do much about your wife's pay at work, nor can you tell her boss to quit working her so hard. You most definitely cannot make the boss appreciate her as much as he or she should.

As a husband, you can make sure your wife does not become overburdened with work at home. You can make sure her pay is commensurate with her work at home by taking her out on dates and relieving her of some work.

Remember the Hundred/ Hundred Proposition

When I was about to get married, the wise old minister who talked to us before the ceremony gave us some advice—I have never forgotten it. First, he told us to never go to bed being angry at each other. We have not always accomplished this, but I would say we have a 99 percent success rate. Second, he told us never to say the word divorce when referring to our marriage or each other. We never have. Finally, he told us that marriage is not fifty/ fifty, but a one hundred/ one hundred proposition. Again, we have not always been one hundred/ one hundred, but I believe we are in the ninetieth percentile on our success in this area. I hope you will take his advice to heart as I did.

If you are not having forty-five minutes of conversation with your wife at one sitting, try it. You will be amazed at her insight on various matters that come up each week. Her solutions to problems are going to be different than yours. Many times they are going to be better. Other times, she will add something that puts a whole new twist on the way you perceive the world, other people and problem solving. That is why men and women were made differently. We see things from different perspectives.

Don't Be Involved in an Unhappy Spiral

I once saw a poster hanging in an office. It said, "If you are grouchy, mean, or worrisome, there will be a ten dollar charge for putting up with you." How rich would your wife be now if she collected ten dollars for every such offense from the time you were married to the present?

Instead of the ten-dollar charge being paid to her for offenses, why not apply it toward your dating fund? Many men pay a lot higher price in child support and alimony. The heartache to each person in a divorce is incomprehensible, not just to the man and woman, but more so to the children. The biggest price of all is when those children pass the heartache on to their wives and children after they are married. They repeat a cycle that seems never ending.

I believe you can reverse this spiral of unhappy marriages and sad people. You will do it by dating your wife and treating her with respect. You will do it by avoiding the word divorce when referring to your marriage and by giving one hundred percent of your efforts to make your marriage a success. Discouragement will be your greatest enemy, persistence your greatest tool.

Be Persistent

Persistence in trying to date your wife should be an important goal in your life. She is the only thing you have committed to for a lifetime. Remember the words, "till death do you part." They were part of the marriage ceremony. Some ceremonies go beyond that and say, "for time and eternity." That is a long time. You were a child for eighteen years. You went to school for twelve years and for an additional four to twelve years if you attended college, etc. You will work at your occupation for twenty to forty years. You have committed to your wife that you will be there for her until the day you die or beyond. That takes persistence.

You must maintain persistence in your attempt at dating your wife. Every date will not work out. Some appointments may be broken. Unpleasant things can happen on dates. But you will remember the happy and exciting moments far after the unpleasant and dull periods fade from your memory.

If you want to know what your wife would like to do on a date, ask her. The most dismal answer on all the questionnaires I had returned to me was from a woman who answered question #25 with the following comment: "My husband and I don't date, we practice being married, not single." She repeatedly answered all the questions, "We don't date, we don't date, we don't date." For her anniversary, she wanted to "win the lottery." My guess is that she probably wanted to win so she could get away from her husband. "What is a savings account?" was her answer to the question, *"How many savings accounts do you have?"* Lastly, to question #95, *"What can your husband do to help you prepare for dates?"* she answered, "Get out of my way." I suspect the divorce is final by now.

That was the only totally negative questionnaire I received. The rest of the wives were comparatively happy but wanted some improvement in their dating lives with their husbands. Most said their husbands were their best friends.

5

Creating New Habits

One day a wife tried to help her husband improve on one of his irritating habits. "Honey, you have one bad habit. You never listen when I am talking to you. You get a faraway look in your eyes, and your mind wanders off. Promise me you will work on that."

The husband responded, "What was that, dear?"

The ideas for success in this book are meant to stimulate action. But first, there are a few more hints that will help you along the way. There are some little things, some basics, gleaned from the pages of the completed questionnaires, which can act as a foundation for your success.

Save Your Money, but Smell the Roses, Too

I must first say a word about money. In future chapters I will say more about money. Right now, consider this: a funny poster I once saw was of a man who looked to be one hundred thirty years old. He had wrinkles on his wrinkles and his skin was hanging from his face and sagging from all his bones. He reminded me of a very old, droopy-skinned hound dog. He had thin, gray hair. To complete the effect, he wore pop-bottle glasses.

It was hard to imagine that there was not some computer enhancement going on here. It just did not seem possible that anyone could look that old. Ironically, he was pictured sitting on a dirt bike motorcycle with both hands on the handle bar grips. The man had an extremely puzzled look on his face. At the bottom of the poster was this caption: "Work hard and save all your money, so when you are old, you can buy things only young people enjoy."

You must save for the future and for your retirement years. However, you need to stop and smell the roses along the way, too. Consider the possibility that you may not be alive when it's time to retire. It is also possible you will not be in good health. There may be other reasons you cannot enjoy your "old age" when the time arrives.

Create Memories for Your Golden Years

A plan to save for the future is sound. So, too, is the plan to use some of your money to build the memories that will carry you into those golden years. Good memories can carry you through many troublesome times. If you have not laid a solid foundation of good memories, your marriage may not endure the midlife crisis period or the hardships that come along.

When you reach the stage in your life when you can sit on the porch in a rocking chair, good memories will make those years much more pleasant. The thought of not accomplishing all the things you wanted to do will not come back to haunt you. If you clutter your life with unfulfilled dreams, you will have regrets. Rocking chairs are for recalling memories after you can no longer create them. Spend a little money to create memories while you still can.

Look into Her Eyes

Next, a word about romance. The most romantic moment I ever had with my wife was one morning a few years ago while we were at the breakfast table. There was a moment while we were talking that I looked up at her and suddenly my eyes met hers. It was as if I could see right into her soul. She had the bluest eyes—deep blue like the waters off the Hawaiian coast. I felt as if I were about to be absorbed right into them. She was beautiful. In an instant, I knew she cared about me way down inside herself. She loved me and that message came right through those big, beautiful, blue eyes.

I tell you this knowing you are going to think my story sounds pretty corny. That is fine. The point is it was her eyes that spoke volumes, not her words. If you will look into your wife's eyes as you interact, I promise many romantic moments. I am not talking about sexual encounters, although romantic moments can progress to that point.

When I say "romantic moments," I mean moments of emotional attraction or aura. Look into her eyes when she talks to you. You will learn much from looking at her, and in return, she will be able to tell that you care by looking into your eyes. She will feel what you are saying. The sound of your words is not as effective as the eye contact and the communication that occurs by looking at each other. The eyes are the windows to the soul.

Conversations Start with a Touch

Your hands are the second most important tools, after the eyes, you have for conveying your love. A woman cannot stay distant long when you are holding her hand or touching her. The surveys showed that the sense of touch is extremely important to a woman. Always try to start a conversation with a touch. If she is standing, walk over to her and put your arms around her. If she is sitting, sit next to her and take her hand in yours, or put your arm around her shoulder. Touch is the door to the body.

Don't Sweat the Trifles

Begin to understand the importance of using all the senses in communicating with your wife. Use sight, speech, touching and hearing. Look into her eyes, talk softly, touch her and listen to her. They seem like little things, trifles, but the little things can make a tremendous difference in your marriage. Thomas Sprat has said, "A great proportion of the wretchedness which has embittered married life, has originated in a negligence of trifles . . ."

I want to give you an example of negligence of trifles. I once went to a family fight, as we call it in police work. This family fight was similar to hundreds of others I had occasion to attend. The fight occurred in a middle-class neighborhood and involved a simple infraction that escalated into an unfortunate incident. It involved a family in which the husband worked as a roofer.

The husband came home from work as usual. He was tired. He had worked in the hot Arizona sun all day. His wife also had been working hard all day doing laundry, cleaning house and preparing a pot of beans in a hot kitchen.

When the husband arrived home, he sat at the dining room table that contained the pot of beans and all the trimmings. As he filled his plate, he noticed that some of the beans were black and burned. The husband said, "Why did you burn the beans?" An argument immediately ensued, and each side defended its position of having worked hard all day to prepare for this time together. Both sides felt the other person had let them down. The husband thought the wife should have prepared a better dinner since he had been working hard all day; the wife thought her husband should have appreciated her for attempting to make a good dinner; she, too, had been working hard all day.

When the argument escalated, the wife decided she was not going to hear any more of her husband's bantering. She got up and left her husband and two children, ages five and eight, still sitting at the table. As she left the room, the husband picked up the pot of beans and threw it across the kitchen, splattering beans on the wall and floor.

Seconds later, he heard his wife coming down the hallway of their home. As she came out of the bedroom, the husband noticed that she had a gun in her hand. He still had his car keys in his pocket, so he ran out the front door toward his car. While he was trying to start the engine, his wife arrived. When she walked up to the open driver's side window, she pressed the gun against her husband's neck and pulled the trigger. As the engine roared to life, the bullet traveled through the man's neck, causing massive trauma.

The husband had enough presence of mind to back out of the driveway and start driving down the residential street that led away from their house. In a few seconds, he realized the seriousness of the wound and pulled the car toward the curb. He opened the car door and collapsed on the grass in a neighbor's front yard, just three houses away from his own.

As the man fell, someone spotted him and called the police. Officers arrested the wife without incident. The man was taken to a local hospital in critical condition, and the children were placed in a state foster home.

This husband and wife made communication an event. All this over a pot of burned beans. A "trifle." Most family arguments are the result of something just as trivial, and some are even more ridiculous. I must tell you that the husband survived and did not press charges against his wife, so the county attorney could not prosecute her (this was before domestic violence laws). When released from the hospital, he moved back into the house with his wife, and soon after that, they moved from the neighborhood.

An old child's poem states:
Beautiful faces are they that wear
The light of a pleasant spirit there;

Beautiful hands are they that do
Deeds that are noble, good and true;
Beautiful feet are they that go
Swiftly to lighten another's woe.
—*Unknown*

What kinds of faces did the participants in this family dispute wear? What kinds of deeds did the hands do? To what kind of actions did their feet lead? What if the husband and wife had applied the message of this child's poem?

Provide Solutions, Not Criticism

Had this couple made communication a process, the scene could have gone like this: The husband comes home tired and hot. He finds the beans burned. Instead of condemning his wife, he smiles and says, "Looks like you've been cooking all day. How would you like to get out of the kitchen? Why don't we all go out to dinner?"

The wife already knows the beans burned. She gladly says, "That's a great idea. I'm sorry the beans burned. After staying up all night with our son who was sick, I was really tired. I guess I dozed off in the chair for a few minutes too long."

The husband replies, "I knew there was a good reason the beans burned. You're usually a great cook, and you work hard as a mother and wife. You deserve to go out. Let me take a quick shower and we'll go."

Now what are the faces, hands and feet doing? Now what kind of spirit prevails in the home? Is this a more pleasant scene? Of course it is. To create this kind of scene is just that simple, too. It comes down to little things such as the husband and wife thinking of each other and wanting to make their time together more pleasant. These thoughts lead to cooperation instead of antagonism.

Listen to the Voice Inside

The poem talks about a "pleasant spirit." I believe there is a spirit, a conscience, a "light," or whatever else you may call it, locked up inside your physical body. The voice is calling quietly, asking for you to listen. Sometimes the voice is so faint you cannot hear it unless you listen closely; however, it is there. The voice will grow stronger and clearer as you listen more intently. Letting that pleasant spirit speak to you will provide a power that may have been missing in your marriage to this point. It is the power that will fill your marriage with success and joy. It can only be heard when you are still and trying to hear it. The voice is inside you. The power is inside you. Listen to the voice. Use the power and have a successful marriage.

Now it is time to turn your thoughts to the ideas that will generate success. I suggest you read all fifty-two ideas in the next chapter. When reading them, picture yourself doing these things. Think them through. Write down other thoughts that come to you as you read—Thought will stimulate action. Once you are finished reading them, go back to the beginning and do them!

Begin with Idea Number One. Do one of these ideas each week for the next year. Some ideas call for a one-time action, such as taking time to plan a trip, etc. Others contain actions that need repeating until they are habitual. (Studies have shown it takes thirty days to create a new habit.) You can work on more than one at a time; however, do not rush on to the next idea before you have given the one you are working on a chance to sink in.

As you begin to take action, your actions will in turn strengthen your thoughts, creating a positive, upward spiral. By following the easy guidelines contained on the following pages, your dreams can come true. Man's search for happiness is never ending.

6

Fifty-two Ideas for Successful Dating and Marital Harmony

A husband should always try to treat his wife with the greatest courtesy and respect, holding her in the highest esteem. He should speak to her in a kind and a soft manner, showing his love by word and deed. As she feels this love and tenderness she will mirror it and return it tenfold.

—James E. Faust

Below is a list of ideas for success with explanations and/or commentary. If you practice these ideas, they will become habits, and will result in your wife becoming more cherished as one of your dominant thoughts.

Not long ago, a friend attended a meeting where the speaker talked of the simple things in relationships. He spoke of husbands opening doors for their spouse and holding hands with her. My friend started doing only these two things. He recently confessed to me that their relationship is better now than it has been in years. He has since added a few other ideas to his dating habits, using them on a rotating basis. He does one thing for a while and then switches to something else to keep her guessing

47

at what he is going to do next. This keeps their marriage fresh. Enjoy and employ these ideas.

Successful Dating Idea Number One:

Schedule fifteen minutes to sit alone with your wife and talk with her.

Talk about her day with no interruption from the television, telephone, children, doorbell, or anything else. During that fifteen minutes, act as if she is the only thing that exists in the universe. Ignore everything else. If you have to, go into a room with her and lock the door. Unplug the telephone or allow the calls to go to your answering machine or voice mail. If you are a television addict, decide which program you can do without. After a few sessions, you will find her asking about your day. When she does, do not let the focus shift entirely to your issues. Increase your sessions to thirty minutes a day, maybe even longer, if you need to. I promise that you will soon love and look forward to this daily time together. Let her do most of the talking. You listen. Soak up what she is saying. Ask her, "How do you feel about that?" Try asking, "What else happened?" Do not offer suggestions unless she asks for them.

If you think you have a solution to the problem she is sharing, bite your tongue. Don't tell her your solution. What she really wants is for you to listen to her. She does not want you to fix her problem when she is directly in the middle of divulging it. Your wife wants you to listen and empathize. She needs you to feel her problem, not fix it. She is relieving stress by talking to you. Do not add to her stress by not listening.

This is one of those times you can hold your wife's hand or put your arm around her to show your support. Most of all, apply the JL (Just Listen) principle. Give her a hug and a kiss after your listening session.

Before marriage, you couldn't wait to be together so you could talk. Cultivate this attitude again and see what rewards you reap in the future. There are dozens of routine things (some unnecessary) that you do for fifteen minutes or more every day. Few are more important than the time you spend listening with an open heart. Make sure your wife gets her time with you. It isn't enough to be physically present. The rewards come when you are mentally and emotionally present as well. Repeat until it is habit. Here it is again. There is no substitute for time spent together.

Successful Dating Idea Number Two:

One day this week, meet your wife during your workday and have lunch together.

Spending some time together in the middle of the day helps you see each other in a different light! This provides both of you with a change, and because you have to eat lunch anyway, this is a way to "dovetail"—to accomplish two things at once.

If the logistics of sharing this meal is a challenge, you may have to be creative. Meet at a midway point, or go into work a little early so you can take a longer lunch hour. If, for some reason, it still will not work to get together for lunch, arrange to spend part of your lunch hour talking to her on the telephone. A phone visit is not as good as an in-person visit during lunch, but it is better than no contact at all.

Successful Dating Idea Number Three:

Hug your wife. Make your hug last at least five to ten seconds before releasing her.

Initiate this strategy today and continue every day from this day forward. It is important. In my survey, women listed cuddling as the number one thing they would like their husbands to do more. A hug, though not quite equal, is a brief form of cuddling. A long hug lets her know you have taken the time to recognize she is there. A one-second hug is like a one-cent tip: it is an insult. A recent study showed that five hugs a day are required for good mental and physical health.

Successful Dating Idea Number Four:

Kiss your wife before going your separate ways every morning. Make the kiss last for five seconds.

This, too, would add much to your marriage if carried out every day. As with a hug, a one-second kiss tells her you do not have time for her. Five or ten-second kisses tell her you love her. It can be sensual without being sexual. When concluding the kiss, look into her eyes and say, "I love you."

One wife recently gave birth to twins. She said her husband agreed to kiss her for ten seconds no matter what was happening with the children. When it's a crazy time with crying and screaming children, a five or ten second kiss lets the two of you know you are connected and important.

Successful Dating Idea Number Five:

Give your wife a five-second kiss when you both are home again in the evening.

This reinforces idea number four. Let her know you are glad to be with her again. Do not give her one of those quick pecks on the cheek and head for the recliner. She has not seen you in several hours. Show her that she matters and that you are the one person in this world who is most concerned about her welfare.

Successful Dating Idea Number Six:

Take your wife out to a movie.

Make the appointment early in the week. Tell her on Monday that you want to take her out to a movie on Friday or Saturday. Anticipation is an important element in dating. The pleasure increases if your wife has a week to think about the time you are going to spend together.

Most wives I surveyed said they enjoy occasional spontaneous dates. There were many comments, however, which suggested wives do not appreciate last-minute surprises when there are arrangements to make. They want to know ahead of time they are going out. They want time to put on makeup, get a baby sitter or reschedule other conflicting appointments.

When you make the appointment with her, also ask her to choose the movie so she will get to see one she will enjoy. If you let her choose the movie, you send her a message that she is important to you and that her opinion counts. It also conveys your trust in her decision. Once she chooses the movie, don't grumble and tell her you want to see something else. Go to the movie she wants this time; next time, you choose. In a good marriage, cooperation abounds. If you give her the choice first and make an effort to enjoy it, she will be likely to accept your choice the next week.

Grumbling about ticket prices or the cost of popcorn and sodas is not to be done. This sends her a signal that she is not worth the price of a ticket or the price of a snack. She is worth infinitely more than ten or fifteen bucks. Don't be cheap. Don't make her feel worthless by grumbling about the prices.

Don't boast about how much you have spent, but say something like: "I'd pay ten times that price for a ticket to see this movie with you tonight." Try saying, "I can't think of anything

I would rather spend money on tonight than seeing a movie with you." Then, give her a kiss right there in front of everybody. Ah, romance. I love it.

While discussing this with one wife, she said, "I don't know too many men who would do that (kiss her in front of other people). I would love it, though."

Successful Dating Idea Number Seven:

Take your wife out to dinner this month.

Spend twenty to fifty dollars for the dinner, not including drinks. Put it on your calendar now so you both can prepare for and anticipate the dinner. Let her choose the restaurant. Again, don't complain about prices. The idea here is to let her know she is worth every penny and more. If she says, "Oh, honey, this costs too much money." Simply say, "You are worth it." Kind of gives you a tingly feeling just thinking about the response you might get, doesn't it?

Successful Dating Idea Number Eight:

Schedule dinner alone with your wife at your house with no interruptions at least once in the coming month.

Take the phone off the hook, do not answer the door, leave the children with neighbors, a relative or baby sitter, and then you cook the meal. Afterward, you can do the dishes together. You can also buy prepared food. Pick it up on the way home from work, or have it delivered. It can be as simple as pizza, or as elaborate as a catered meal. Candlelight and soft music are good mood makers. Be alone and enjoy each other.

Successful Dating Idea Number Nine:

Rent a good video, take it home, and watch it together.

As with Idea Number Eight, ignore a ringing phone or doorbell. Have someone watch your children so you can be alone. Have the popcorn, candy, sodas or other enjoyable snacks available at show time. Turn out the lights. A television can give off a romantic glow almost as suitable as lighted candles.

Successful Dating Idea Number Ten:

Take your wife for an overnight stay at a great hotel in the next three months.

Select a hotel that is at least fifty miles from your house, if possible. Call and make reservations now, and clear your calendars so nothing interferes with that overnight rendezvous. If possible, make it a two-night mini-vacation. (One wife wrote, "This is just the right amount of time away.") Make reservations for a hotel room, dinner, arrange for a baby sitter, and service the car in advance. It is not good to arrive at the day before the trip after three months of anticipation and discover you cannot go because of an overlooked detail.

Successful Dating Idea Number Eleven:

Take a walk with your wife tonight.

This only requires passing up a half-hour television show. You might find yourself doing most of the talking during this walk, or she might talk to you. When the moon and stars are out, it's a great time to walk. Choose a safe area. You might want to stop and relax on some grass along your route and talk.

Successful Dating Idea Number Twelve:

Spend time together to schedule what you are going to do and where you are going to go for your next anniversary.

Anniversaries are the perfect time to renew marriage vows and reintroduce romance. Make the reservations now, if required. As suggested above, make sure that as time draws nearer, all arrangements are in order so there are no glitches. The logistics needs to go as smoothly as possible so you both can enjoy the time together.

Successful Dating Idea Number Thirteen:

Spend time together to decide where you are going to go for your next five-year anniversary, whether that be your fifth, tenth, fifteenth, twentieth, twenty-fifth, thirtieth, etc.

Make each five-year anniversary even more special. Plan to make these occasions that you will look forward to and create rewarding memories that you will share. Start putting money in a savings account designated for that trip. Estimate the cost of this trip. Figure the number of paychecks you will receive between now and your trip. Put an amount of money in the bank each time you receive a paycheck. When you reach the date for your five-year anniversary trip to take place, you will have the money to go.

Don't take the money out of this account except in case of impending bankruptcy or a life-and-death situation. That may sound a little stringent, but these getaways will be well worth resisting the temptation to dip into your savings. Investing in a five-year anniversary trip will bring great dividends.

Gadgets and toys wear out over time, but the memories you have will stay with you forever. Make some good ones. If you simply cannot afford a five-year trip (or choose to go somewhere that is quite expensive), make it a ten-year trip. Save your money as recommended, but spread it out over ten years. Even a trip every ten years is better than never going anywhere special together.

My wife and I went to San Diego, California for our fifth anniversary. We took a trip to Germany, Austria and France for our tenth. For our fifteenth anniversary, we went to Alaska and stayed in a fishing lodge. The lodge hired a renowned chef who prepared delicious meals every day. Fishing guides took us out on the Kenai River for two days. We took a fly-in trip to a wilderness lake one day and halibut fishing on the ocean another day. For our twentieth anniversary, we traveled to Hawaii and stayed one block from Waikiki Beach for a week and toured the island of Oahu from one end to the other. For our twenty-fifth anniversary, we took a Caribbean cruise. My wife loves lighthouses, so for our thirtieth anniversary we are going to drive either the Atlantic or Pacific coast and see as many lighthouses as we can for a couple of weeks.

Again, resolve details in advance. When we went to Hawaii, I planned on driving to the airport and loaded our luggage in the trunk of our car. At the last minute, we decided to have someone else drive our car and drop us off. I left my keys on the counter at home since I would not need them in Hawaii. Our driver used a spare set of keys to start the car and we excitedly headed off to the airport. When we arrived at the curbside luggage check-in station, I walked to the trunk of the car to retrieve the luggage and found the spare keys did not include a trunk key.

All our luggage was in the trunk of the car except my carry-on bag. I jumped in the car and started for home to get the trunk key. Halfway home, I saw in my rearview mirror a State Highway Patrol car with the red lights flashing. I was driving way over the speed limit. When I pulled over, he kept going. Whew! Again, I headed toward home, but soon realized I would never make it and would miss my flight if I continued. I turned around and sped back to the airport to find my wife so she would not go to Hawaii alone.

My wife was at the boarding gate, anxiously awaiting my return. We boarded the plane at the last second, and my wife asked about our luggage. I turned to her, smiled, and said, "It's our anniversary. We don't need clothes. Why do we need luggage?"

When we arrived in Hawaii, I called and asked my daughter to get the key to the trunk. She took our luggage to the air express office and shipped it on the next available flight. The next afternoon, my wife and I went to the airport and picked up our bags. Until then, we had the clothes on our backs, my carry-on bag with some books in it, and each other. It was great! We laugh about this every time we think about it. It was the first time in twenty years we shared the same toothbrush (my wife purchased it at a little store at the condominium where we stayed). Try not to overlook details, but if you do, don't let them ruin your trip. It will seem funny when you look back, so laugh and enjoy it now.

Successful Dating Idea Number Fourteen:

Order flowers for your wife for no reason at all.

Mark it on your calendar now. Better yet, call the florist right now. Have flowers delivered to your home or to her place of work. If you cannot afford to order flowers, pick some wild flowers at a park or beside the road, or get them out of your yard. Ring the doorbell and deliver them to her. If you decide to pick them and not buy them, it's all right. She will love them just like they are. Here, it's the flowers that count, not the price tag.

Successful Dating Idea Number Fifteen:

Buy your wife her favorite box of chocolates.

A small box will do. Here again, it's not the size of the box, but putting the thought into action that counts. If you have no idea what her favorite chocolate is, ask her. If she doesn't like chocolate, select a special pastry or other gourmet dessert. To surprise her, you can ask other women you know what they like and try that. If she does not like the type you choose, try another kind next time until you get it right.

Successful Dating Idea Number Sixteen:

Open the car door for your wife each time you go somewhere together.

Where the weather is severe, this suggestion may need modifying. For example, in Arizona, when the temperature is one hundred ten degrees, the temperature can range up to two hundred degrees inside the car. Let your wife remain inside the air-conditioned building until you get the air-conditioning going in the car. Drive to the door and pick her up after the car has cooled down a little. If you live in Minnesota and its winter . . . well, you get the idea.

Unlike throwing your coat down over a puddle, this is a practice that should still be very much in fashion. It is a way for you to feel greater togetherness since you relate to your wife each time she gets in and out of the car. Offer her your hand, look into her eyes, and say something to her each time she gets in or out.

Successful Dating Idea Number Seventeen:

Open doors to buildings for your wife.

Think of it as a way to exercise your biceps if you must, but don't neglect this action. Over ninety-five percent of the women surveyed said they want their husbands to extend this courtesy. When I decided to put this practice back into my marriage, I discovered something interesting: my wife walked faster than me. She would always reach the door first. So, I started holding her hand as we walked. Now we arrive at the door together. Then, I can gently pull back on her hand. She stops, and I reach for the door handle first.

Successful Dating Idea Number Eighteen:

Hold hands with your wife when you walk together in public.

By deciding to open doors for my wife, I ended up holding her hand more often. This simple act can create amazing bonds between you and your wife. Not only that, it is a good way to display to your children and to others around you that you enjoy marriage. Wives reported they felt more secure, more loved and more special when their husbands held their hand. I believe one reason they suggested that this action made them feel special is that so few husbands do this. If you will start, she will consider you unique and be grateful that you are a step ahead of other husbands.

Successful Dating Idea Number Nineteen:

Put your arm around your wife when you sit together.

You can do this anytime, whether you are at home, at a friend's house, or in a public place such as a theater. You can even do this in church and no one will complain. You don't have to leave your arm around her shoulders until it goes to sleep, but remember, women like cuddling.

Successful Dating Idea Number Twenty:

Take a break at work and call your wife to tell her you love her.

This is a treat for your wife. When she knows you took time out of your busy day to call to say you were thinking about her, it makes her feel good. It also causes her to think about you and remember what a great man she is married to!

One woman who responded to the survey said the only reason her husband calls her from work is so he can ask her to do something. Occasionally, those kinds of calls are necessary. That husband (and every other husband) should call occasionally to express his love and concern without asking for anything. If you will learn to call her for no reason, your wife will be happier to respond when you do request her help.

Successful Dating Idea Number Twenty-one:

Tell your wife you love her at least five times today.

That may seem like a lot, but you may need to make up for all the days you haven't said, "I love you." Besides, your wife never tires of hearing a sincere expression of love. When you tell her you love her, don't just say it in passing. Stop, look into her eyes, and say the words with meaning, using the tone and inflection that are proper for the moment. There is a big difference between walking toward the door with your back to your wife while saying "I love you" over your shoulder versus stopping and planting your feet, turning toward her, making eye contact, and saying one word at a time, "I–love–you."

Successful Dating Idea Number Twenty-two:

Cuddle with your wife on the couch tonight.

Instead of sitting in a chair or recliner on the opposite side of the room, sit with your wife on the couch. Hold her hand or put your arm around her. This physical closeness creates a feeling of unity between you. It helps her feel wanted. It assures her that you will touch and hold her other than when you are in the bedroom. She will love you for it and will fondly remember those nights sitting with you.

Successful Dating Idea Number Twenty-three:

Spend an equal amount of money on your wife this month as you do on yourself.

Pay attention to the amount of money you spend on yourself this month and make sure you are spending an equal amount on your wife. Don't be selfish; she deserves as much as you do. If you have to decrease the amount you spend on yourself, then so be it. In the survey, eighty percent of the wives remarked that their husbands spent more money on themselves than on them. Ten percent reported their husbands spent an equal amount on them and ten percent said their husbands spent more on the wives than on themselves.

Where do you fall in this category? Be honest with yourself. (A good way to determine if you are being fair is to ask your wife.) Pay attention to your spending habits in the future.

Successful Dating Idea Number Twenty-four:

Ask your wife what activities you now do alone that she would like to participate in, such as golfing, fishing, hunting, tennis, etc.

Over half the women surveyed said they wished their husband would take them along when he did "his thing." Until I conducted this survey, I never knew how many women wanted to learn how to golf. If you are a golfer, ask your wife if she wants to go with you. If she does go with you, be patient. Be generous, allow your wife plenty of Mulligan's (if needed), and above all, have fun.

If your "thing" is not golf, ask your wife if she wants to participate in an activity you enjoy. My hobby was fishing, especially bass fishing. I fished mostly in tournaments. When we were first married, we spent many weekends fishing for trout in the cool pine country of Arizona. When we started having children, I switched to bass fishing and she switched to staying home. It never occurred to me that she would still want to go fishing. She seemed to be perfectly content staying home with the children until one day she expressed interest in a husband-wife bass tournament series.

We entered a tournament, and we won some money. When we went again, she caught the second biggest fish and we finished second place in the tournament. Another second place finish came to us at a subsequent tournament. That year, we won some money. We also obtained some trophy plaques that still hang in our family room. We made it to the championship tournament, and we had a great time doing it. That big fish she caught is in my thoughts quite often. I was then, and still am, very proud of her.

Successful Dating Idea Number Twenty-five:

Open a special checking account that you will use solely for dating your wife.

This is important. If you have not done so already, open a savings account and set aside money for your anniversary celebrations and your vacations together. Put money into this account regularly and you'll save enough for great anniversary dates and trips. Our anniversary this year was spent at a 250 dollar per night resort in Sedona, Arizona.

We had the money because we paid off our credit cards. We also put my pocket change in a piggy bank every night and saved money out of each of our checks each week. Please read the chapter entitled "Money and Dating" and look for your own way to find extra money to use for dates. It's easier than you think. Four quarters a day for one year can add up to a $365 resort anniversary.

Successful Dating Idea Number Twenty-six:

Tell your wife a joke today and each day after this.

Buy a joke book at a bookstore. Listen for good, clean jokes at work or among your friends. Come home with a joke each day if possible. In the survey, wives listed failure to listen and converse and failure to laugh as common points of concern about their husbands. One wife wrote, "He used to be so funny before we were married; what happened?"

Successful Dating Idea Number Twenty-seven:

Pray or meditate together.

Several wives listed this on their survey. Women seem to have an easier time getting in touch with their spiritual side than do men. The old saying, "The family that prays together, stays together," is just as reliable now.

My wife and I took an eight-week course from a marriage counselor last year to conduct research for this book. Taking the class didn't hurt anything in our personal relationship, either. The subject of prayer came up in a session. The consensus among the other five couples attending was that when the husband and wife prayed together, everything seemed to progress much more smoothly in their homes.

I have since talked to scores of women about this subject. Almost invariably, when there is trouble in the home, there is no prayer in the home. When I conversed with happy wives, I asked about prayer in the home. Most of the time there is some personal worship being done by the couple. What can a little prayer, a moment of silence, or thoughtful meditation hurt?

Successful Dating Idea Number Twenty-eight:

Have pictures taken of your wife, and carry one with you.

This is an easy one, but one so important. You can put her picture on your desk. Hang it from your rear view mirror. I hang one from a clip in my locker at work. Put her picture in a place where you will see it every day. Let it remind you why you exist. You exist for her, and she exists for you. I am happier when I see her picture in my locker at the end of an otherwise rotten day.

The picture can also remind you that she is your "one and only." You are married; you should not be entertaining thoughts about other women. Infidelity is a top cause of divorce. Let the picture remind you that you are happily married.

Successful Dating Idea Number Twenty-nine:

Stop on the way home from work, buy her favorite fruit or sweet treat, and take it home to her.

This is one of those little thoughtful things that are so easy to do and yet seem to mean so much to a wife. Recently, I was standing by a vending machine. My wife likes Junior Mints and there was a package in the machine. Plugging the machine with the fifty cents required for the purchase was easy. The box went home with me and I left it beside her purse. I left a short note that simply said, "These are for you, honey." I got a big kiss after she found them, and I thought she was going to cry when she said, "That was so sweet." All this over a small box of Junior Mints. Wow!

How difficult can it be to take a few minutes to do a thoughtful thing for your wife? Is it that troublesome to spare fifty cents or a dollar? You will be happy you tried this idea.

Successful Dating Idea Number Thirty:

Fix something around the house.

There are always squeaky doors needing oil, pictures to hang, or painting to do. Maybe you have a roof that leaks or some other chore waiting on that "honey do" list. Do one (or even two) of those things this weekend. You will free yourself from that chore hanging over your head. You will be happy with your wife's response to the chore being completed.

Successful Dating Idea Number Thirty-one:

Leave work early one day this week. Tell your wife you want to go somewhere special, and you are taking a few hours off work for her.

This will mean a lot to her. Most likely there have been times when you have worked longer hours or when your work seemed to come first. Reverse the tables. One day this week, show her that time with her is important to you. This is big in her book. Quitting work early for her is big. Wanting to go somewhere with her when you get off early is big. Make this even more memorable: tell her the day before that you are going to do this, and let her know what time you are going to be home. Then, take her to a special, expensive restaurant.

Successful Dating Idea Number Thirty-two:

Massage her back.

Give her a massage with no sex afterward unless she initiates it. Close your eyes, if you have to. Force yourself to think platonic thoughts. This is for her, not you. (This is bigger than getting off work early.) If you can do this for her, I think you have taken a huge step toward being a very good husband.

Successful Dating Idea Number Thirty-three:

Take a nap together Sunday afternoon.

Help get the children's needs taken care of, or help your wife with her responsibilities so you can take a nap together. This suggestion came from several surveys. Taking a nap together is one of those little things that a wife appreciates and enjoys. Napping seems to go along with cuddling. It is one more opportunity to be close to your wife without requiring something from her. Take the nap; you need the break. I used to detest naps, but after reading this suggestion on many surveys, I forced myself to try. Now I'm glad the surveys mentioned it, and I look forward to that quiet, peaceful time together.

Successful Dating Idea Number Thirty-four:

Wash the dishes with your wife.

Washing dishes together gives the two of you a few minutes to talk and relate. It is also a time you can provide assistance. Wives like to know they can count on their husbands for some help. This is especially true when the family is bigger and your wife's responsibilities are large. You are your wife's helper, so help. One of you can wash the dishes; the other can dry. Even better, let her sit back and relax and talk to you while you wash the dishes and give her a break. Whichever way you choose to do this, it is the togetherness that is important. A wife advised, "Some men feel that once they make a good living (dollar-wise), they no longer need to help out at home." Not so!

Successful Dating Idea Number Thirty-five:

Make the bed for her.

You sleep in it, too, so make it! If you prefer, make the bed together. One person on each side makes this about a one-minute job or less. The thing to remember here is this: making the bed is not exclusively your wife's job. I promise this action will not diminish your masculinity. Unfortunately, though I say that humorously, many of us still have strong stereotypes of what is the man's responsibility and what is the woman's. Wake up on the right side of the bed and make it!

Successful Dating Idea Number Thirty-six:

Touch her when you talk to her.

Take her by the hand, put your arm around her waist or her shoulders, and pull her close. Any kind of touching during the process of communicating helps show her you care and shows you are really paying attention and not just patronizing her. This brings the two of you closer, physically and emotionally.

Successful Dating Idea Number Thirty-seven:

Play "footsy" with her under the table.

This is not "kid stuff." It's a way to flirt with your wife. It's great. I like it. My wife likes it, and more than one wife wrote about it on the survey. Flirting with your wife is fun.

Successful Dating Idea Number Thirty-eight:

Put the seat down.

This is definitely not in the same category as playing "footsy," but this one-second action is one your wife may be looking forward to. It does not use very many calories, however, so for those of you on a diet, this is not the fat burner you would like it to be; it is just too easy. Enough said?

Successful Dating Idea Number Thirty-nine:

Pick up your clothes.

They are your clothes. Don't relegate your wife to being a slave. Don't treat her like your mother. Help your wife. She helps you. If you have a wife that does not help you, try this for a while, and she might start. This is reciprocity.

Successful Dating Idea Number Forty:

Write your wife a love letter and mail it to her.

This may take a little thought, but I know you can express your feelings in writing. It does not have to be elaborate, so just write from your heart. It will be a cherished thing in your wife's eyes. Chances are, she will put it in a safe place and keep it forever. Your wife can be sentimental. You can also, if you try.

Just think: after you are dead and gone and she is still here, she will open her special little box, take out this letter and read it again. If she precedes you, you'll find she treasured your words. You'll be glad you expressed them when she could still hear and see your love.

Successful Dating Idea Number Forty-one:

Bring your wife a cold drink (or a glass of something warm on a cold evening).

How many times has she brought you a drink while you were reading the newspaper or watching television? Return the favor. While you are at it, you might as well get a drink for yourself, and then sit—and sip—together.

Successful Dating Idea Number Forty-two:

Look in her eyes when the two of you are talking together.

As a child, you may remember your parents saying, "Look at me when I'm talking to you." They wanted to be sure you were paying attention to what they were saying. They also wanted you to learn that it is discourteous to not give people your full attention when they are speaking to you. Treat your wife with courtesy. Show her you respect her and are interested in what she has to say. Looking into someone's eyes can be extremely romantic. This is something your mother or father probably never mentioned.

Successful Dating Idea Number Forty-three:

Talk softly to her today.

A technique of communication taught at the Police Academy was to talk softly when someone else is screaming. The screaming person has to listen to hear you when you are talking softly. They cannot hear if they continue yelling.

Talking softly also affects another person. To show concern, caring and love toward the other person, speak softly. Yelling agitates. Talking quietly calms.

Successful Dating Idea Number Forty-four:

Say complimentary things about your wife to others when she is present.

Find an occasion this week when you and your wife are with another couple or a group of people to pay her a public compliment. It can be quite simple, such as "Susan fixed the greatest dinner the other night." It can also be something spectacular, such as "Susan won the Mrs. America pageant the other night, and I am so proud of her."

In language we men can understand, these are home runs and touchdowns in the game of marriage. This idea of praising your wife in front of others is as old as the earth. Greek, Roman, Jewish and Chinese literature records examples of this.

The wise man will truly praise his wife and say every commendable thing about her that he can when in front of others.

Others admire a man with a wonderful wife. A husband who puts down his wife only puts down himself.

Praise her and you magnify yourself without looking like an egotist. As this book will discuss later, "treating her badly in front of others" impairs your relationship. Sarcasm is funny sometimes, but not when it comes to talking about your wife. It's a taboo any husband would do well to observe.

Successful Dating Idea Number Forty-five:

Leave a flower and/or a love note on her pillow.

This is a gift that keeps on giving. It will most likely become another addition to your wife's box of sentimental stuff. From time to time she will take the box out. The flower petals will have fallen off and the paper will have yellowed, but the empty stem and the faded words will still remind her how "sweet" you are.

Successful Dating Idea Number Forty-six:

Dance with her at home.

Occasionally, when a song I like comes on the radio, I will go and find my wife. If she is not in the middle of something important, I will take her in my arms and dance with her for a minute or two. Don't underestimate the power of a short dance to enhance romance (see—I'm not only a dancer, I'm a poet). To my wife's chagrin, I do not dance in public. These short, private dances are the best I can muster. She smiles and sometimes hums to the music as we dance.

Successful Dating Idea Number Forty-seven:

Fix breakfast and serve your wife in bed on her birthday or on Mother's Day.

If you have children, let them help. Your wife will love it and your children will, too. A wife and mother deserve this treatment from time to time—much more often than we seem inclined to offer it. Don't forget to clean up the kitchen when you are done. Don't leave it for her to do. That would spoil the treat.

Successful Dating Idea Number Forty-eight:

Turn out all the lights tonight and listen to your wife's favorite music.

This is usually peaceful, quiet, and romantic. Let the music take the two of you away from your everyday cares and concerns. Talk softly if you want, but only if she initiates it. Light a candle or two and just listen to the music. Take your shoes off. Relax. Enjoy.

Successful Dating Idea Number Forty-nine:

Go to brunch.

This is one of my wife's favorite things to do, and several other wives mentioned it on their questionnaires. Sleep late one Saturday and then get up and go to brunch before you begin your day's activities. Since you have to eat anyway, brunch is an inexpensive, relaxing way to start your day together.

Successful Dating Idea Number Fifty:
Go out for dessert.

While women may prefer brunch, this is one of my favorite things to do. This is for times you can't think of anything else, or at the end of a hectic day. I enjoy going to the dozens of different ice cream shops, pie places or dessert diners. The options are endless. You can easily grow fat and happy together doing this.

Successful Dating Idea Number Fifty-one:

Visit a children's hospital or a rest home.

I cannot leave this section without encouraging you to do something together for someone else. Serving others is a fantastic way to grow closer as a couple.

Helping someone less fortunate than you can aid you in remembering how well off you are. You will find less to complain about. It will give you greater appreciation for your life and your wife.

Successful Dating Idea Number Fifty-two:

Watch a sunset together.

Drive to a spot that has a good view without buildings, power poles or other manufactured objects in the way. Select a spot where the two of you can be alone. Play some good music on the way there. Take a portable radio or keep the car engine running so you can continue to play soft music while the sun goes down. You might even want to dance (you don't need to be Fred Astaire—simply hold each other and sway to the music). Peace and tranquility should prevail. This would also be a good time to pray or meditate together.

Review at the End of the Year

At the conclusion of a year, review the fifty-two success ideas to see if there are areas you are neglecting. Redouble your efforts. Set new goals for the next year or quarter. You might have to try some ideas again if they are not yet habits. At the end of a year, you should be doing some things without even thinking about them. These include such things as holding your wife's hand in public, opening the car or building doors or telling her you love her several times every day. You should be hugging and kissing her daily.

The total expenditure for doing each of the success ideas once in a year is approximately two hundred dollars (not counting the quarterly date, anniversary date or five-year trip). You can do many of them repeatedly without adding to the cost. That is a meager investment for such a priceless person and for a relationship so valuable. I hope you consider your marriage to be worth that much and much more. I encourage you to apply these ideas for dating your wife more frequently. John Wesley said it best: "Do all the good you can; In all the ways you can; In all the places you can; At all the times you can; To all the people you can; As long as ever you can."

I recommend that you "do all the good you can," beginning with your own wife in your own home, "in all the ways you can . . . as long as ever you can." Small acts of goodness are the seeds of a satisfying harvest.

In the coming chapters, you will find lists of ideas for dates. When the wives filled out the surveys, they often listed the same dates under two or more question headings. Sometimes, one wife would put an answer under one question and another wife would put the same answer under a different question. If you see the same answers in different chapters, don't worry about it. It's an opportunity for twice the fun.

7

Choose to Be an Excellent Husband

We are what we repeatedly do.
Excellence, then, is not an act but a habit.
—Aristotle

In this age of fax-on-demand, instant breakfast and drive-through wedding chapels, we have come to expect instantaneous change. As if life was a giant sitcom, we want things resolved in thirty minutes. Some things do happen quickly. Excellence, however, is not achieved quickly.

Becoming a husband requires only a simple ceremony. A minister, Justice of the Peace, or other legally endowed person says a few words, asks a few questions and then pronounces you a husband. However, becoming an excellent husband requires a lifetime of endeavor. It is a process.

Pursue Excellence in Your Marriage

The pursuit of excellence in every undertaking has marked the human race for centuries. In the last fifty years alone, advancements in science, medicine, aeronautics, communication and manufacturing have exceeded all of mankind's previous accomplishments combined. How did we make such great strides forward in such a short span of time? Certain individuals dedicated themselves to a process of education, preparation and persistence.

I believe you can make the same great strides in your marriage as those remarkable individuals achieved in science, medicine, aeronautics, communication and manufacturing. You can make a dramatic difference in your wife's life. You can make a difference in the lives of others. Everything in life is a choice. I believe this to the very core of my soul. Excellence is not an accident. In any endeavor, when enough effort is applied toward a worthwhile goal, excellence results. When greater effort is exerted, greater excellence follows. True excellence is a habit. True excellence is a choice.

I am not saying that you will be an excellent husband by simply doing one or a few of these things suggested in this book, but it's a beginning. Ask your wife to read many of the suggestions listed in this book, and discuss those she would like to do. Then the two of you together should add other ideas.

Choose to Elevate Your Performance

As a husband, you have a choice of being less than average, average, or superior. You can choose the category you fall into. Only by making a choice to do better than you are now doing is it possible to elevate your performance. The plan is simple and will take you to whatever levels you envision and work for.

Abraham Lincoln said it well, "Always bear in mind that your own resolution to succeed is more important than any [other] thing."

8

Thoughts Beget Action

One of the first requirements for any success is to understand that the human mind . . . is capable of any success. However, just half-a-mind is not very effective . . . Any real accomplishment requires a mind that has been fully made up, fully disciplined, effectively focused, powerfully motivated and set on fire with a great purpose and full enthusiasm. In order to make the best and the most of our lives, the law of success requires us to invest our whole minds and our whole souls and our whole selves in our own destiny. No obstacle can for long obstruct the path of a . . . whole-minded person.
—Sterling W. Sill

Your Dating Habits Reflect Your Thoughts

It makes no difference where you are on the continuum. Investing your whole mind, soul and self will bring success. Whether you are enjoying smooth sailing or your marriage is on the rocks, forward movement comes about in the same way. Improving your marriage requires creating new habits. Behind every habit is a series of acts.

Thoughts are the seeds of actions. With your thoughts centered only on your career and your activities at the office, you will spend all your time in business-related activities. You may

75

end up a very successful "breadwinner" with no wife to take the bread home to!

If you want to improve your hook shot, or shave a few minutes off your marathon time, you will think constantly about the goal and practice it until it is a reality. As you begin to think more about your wife, contemplate her needs and wants, and mentally practice ways to meet those needs, your actions will automatically follow. Rewards come on the heels of action. As your positive actions toward her increase, her admiration of you and passion for you will increase.

Your dating habits are a manifestation of your thoughts. If you are like most husbands, dating has slipped from your mind, or at least slipped to a less prominent place in your mind. New dating habits and actions will come as you contemplate the many possibilities for spending and enjoying time with your wife.

Pick Up a Pen

If you have not already done so, before you read any further, I suggest you pick up a pen. It is time to make this book your own. As you progress through the rest of this book, ideas will come to you. Use the margins to write your thoughts and impressions. Cross out the suggestions you are definitely not going to use. Circle those you want to try and put a star beside those you like best. The "Fifty-two Ideas for Successful Dating" have started you thinking about specific actions you can take each day, week, or month. By using them you will move your relationship with your wife to a higher, more loving and passionate level.

You Are What You Repeatedly Do

During my twenty years as a police officer, I had several good supervisors who taught me how to do my job. One in particular, P. T. Landry, was my sergeant for several years. I learned more about police work from him than from any other individual during my career. The men who worked for him affectionately called him P. T., or just Sarge. P. T. was great at what he did.

He had a saying that I heard him reiterate several times: "You play like you practice." This was P. T.'s modernized way of putting Aristotle's "We are what we repeatedly do." Almost every day he would come in, sit at the head table in our briefing room, and start the day by presenting a hypothetical situation. He would say something like:

"You are driving down the street in your patrol car and you see this skuzzy-looking guy pushing a lawn mower out of a garage. You know the people who live there, and this guy is not one of them. What are you going to do?"

Since we were a training squad, P. T.'s questions were usually directed toward a rookie on the squad. Regardless of what the rookie said, P. T. would add several twists and turns. He would enhance the scenario by throwing in another suspect, a weapon, screaming victims, children taken as hostages by the suspect, etc. He could usually tie the rookie up in a little package. But by doing this, the rookie learned (as did the rest of us) how a situation could change from one second to the next. No two experiences are ever alike.

The point is that by thinking through the situations that P. T. gave us every day we learned dozens of solutions to dozens of problems. All these problems were fictitious. However, I came across most of them in real-life situations later. Because P. T. had used fictitious situations to force us to think through things that could happen, I knew the solutions when I had to face similar problems later. A quotation from the Civil War era illustrates this principle: ". . . no man becomes suddenly different from his habit and cherished thought" (Joshua L. Chamberlain, General Commander, Union Forces, Battle of Gettysburg).

Your "Cherished Thoughts" Create Your Actions

General Chamberlain was talking about habits. You have habits you do not label as such. Habits are those automatic responses you have, or your unconscious repetition of the same events every day. These automatic responses and unconscious repetitions are "you." You can change. As Chamberlain points out, it is "cherished thought" which creates action.

You are in the habit of treating your wife a certain way. You are probably unaware of your habits toward her. The only way to change those habits is to make it a habit to think of her frequently during your day.

When you first wake up, think of her and give her a hug or kiss before getting out of bed. Think of her when you are finished shaving, etc. and put away your toiletries. Think of her as you are eating and thank her for her help in preparing the meal. Think of her when you are finished eating, and help her clear the table. Think of her as you are getting ready for work, and put away your pajamas. Think of her as you leave for work, and give her another good hug and kiss. Think of your wife during the day, and call her to tell her you were thinking about her. Make her one of your dominant thoughts. One morning when you roll over to kiss her, she just might grab you and ask you not to leave just yet. Imagine that!

Alter Your Destiny By Altering Your Thoughts

William James said, "The greatest discovery of my generation is that human beings can alter their lives by altering their attitudes of mind." Dr. Dennis R. Deaton says, in his seminars, "We alter our destiny by altering our thoughts."

In brief, a dominant thought is a thought that occupies a frequent and regular place in your conscious mind. By managing those thoughts, you begin to manage your outcomes. Ralph Waldo Emerson said, "A man is what he thinks about all day long." Think about your wife. Make her a dominant thought. Change your destiny and you will change hers.

Thought is the key. By managing your thoughts and giving your wife a dominant place in your conscious mind, you will change the course of your marriage. I challenge you to take this noble action. What manner of man will you be?

A revolution can begin with you. You can create a new, more loving relationship that can last forever.

There are two roads available for you to travel when you are finished with this book. The worst thing you can do after reading this book is to do nothing. Taking that road will cause regret.

The other road available to you as you study these pages will cause you much joy. That road leads to change. I sincerely hope that when you have finished this book you can say, in the words of William Shakespeare, "Presume not that I am the thing I was."

9

Dating and Money

There are two ways of being happy. We may either diminish our wants or augment our means — either will do — the result is the same and it is for each man to decide for himself and do that which happens to be the easiest. If you are idle or sick or poor, however hard it may be to diminish your wants, it will be harder to augment your means. If you are active and prosperous or young or in good health, it may be easier for you to augment your means than to diminish your wants. But if you are wise, you will do both at the same time, young or old, rich or poor, sick or well; and if you are very wise you will do both in such a way as to augment the general happiness of society.
—*Benjamin Franklin*

That is the secret to happiness. Benjamin Franklin started not by telling us how to be rich, but how to be happy. The odd thing is, this is also the way to become wealthy. If you stop spending your money, you have money. When you start earning more money, you have more money.

Pay Now So You Won't Have to Pay Later

When you spend that money on others, it creates more happiness. The first person you should endow with some of your money is your wife. This will create happiness for both of you.

81

Consider the moral of the following story. A minister had to officiate at a funeral. Before he could give the eulogy, he talked to the widow to see what she would like him to say about her departed husband. He asked the sixty-nine-year-old woman what she remembered about the time she spent with her husband.

She replied, "I remember going to the bank every Friday when he got paid." The minister asked, "But what did you do together?" The widow said, "We went to the bank every Friday." "But," the minister said, beginning to get frustrated, "What did you do after you went to the bank?" The widow stated, "We went home, and he recorded the deposit in the savings passbook." The minister, now a bit perplexed, persisted, "But what special memories do you have of things you did together? I must tell the congregation something of your relationship with your dear husband."

The widow, even more perplexed than the minister, looked the minister straight in the eye and replied, "Tell them we went to the bank every Friday after he got paid. That is what we did. I am going to use some of the money to bury him. We have several hundred thousand dollars in the bank, but we never had enough money to do anything together."

They never had enough money to do anything together? What will your wife remember of you when you are gone? Maybe she is not as lucky as the widow. Possibly, you do not even take her to deposit the money. Her memory of you may be that you came home every Friday and told her you had already deposited the money. The flip side of this coin is if you go home and tell your wife you already spent the money and there is none left to deposit.

Whether you are married or not, there is something you probably consider worse than death, and that is divorce. The emotional toll is tremendous. The financial burden can be staggering. In case you have not checked lately, divorce is expensive in the extreme! Fifty percent of all marriages end in divorce. Fortunately, this also means fifty percent of all marriages do not end in divorce. Fifty/ fifty sounds quite good when it comes to gambling, but you should not be gambling when it comes to marriage. This book is to help you beat the odds. It is to help you tip the scales in your favor.

There used to be a commercial on television you may have seen. It showed a mechanic touting the advantages of a particular brand of motor oil. He explained that regular oil changes would increase the chances that your car would run well for many years. At the end of the commercial he said, "You can pay me now, or you can pay me later."

Your wife is not a car. She is infinitely more valuable. She is priceless. I hope you "pay" her now, so you do not have to "pay" her later. I am not talking about much money, as you will see as you progress through this book.

Dating Doesn't Always Have to Cost Money

The most important thing you need to know is that dating never has to cost money. There are many things to do that do not cost money. However, if you are to be happier in your dating, you must revert to what Benjamin Franklin said earlier. If you are very wise, you will diminish your wants so you will have more money. You will also augment your income so you have more money. Then you will bestow some of that money on others, specifically, in your case, on your wife.

Use Credit Cards for Convenience, Not for Loans

I caution you to not go into debt to date your wife, even for your five-year trips. Earn the money or diminish your wants, but do not go into debt through borrowing, whether it is by loans or credit cards. Credit cards are fine to use on a trip, but pay the card off each month. If you have the money saved in the bank to pay off the credit card when the bill comes, you can enjoy the trip without worrying about money. You should use a credit card for convenience, not as a loan.

The most important stuff in life is not stuff. The following advice is probably going to go against all of your current habits. Do not buy stuff with your money! What is stuff? It's just about everything. Particularly, it is everything you do not need.

You do need a car, but consider the consequences of the purchase. When you buy a car for twenty thousand dollars, your twenty thousand dollars is gone. How long does it take you to earn twenty thousand dollars? Look at your pay stub. Not at the gross amount, but the net. Answer the question again, "How long does it take to earn twenty thousand dollars?" Let me throw something else at you. We are not talking about twenty thousand dollars. For a five-year loan, we are talking about twenty-five thousand dollars after interest has been added.

Then, there is the maintenance. Just an oil change every three months costs four hundred dollars over the five-year period. If there are other mechanical problems, just tack them onto the price of the car. Then, there is insurance. If you carry full coverage, as you should, you are looking at another four thousand five hundred dollars for five years. You will definitely buy another set of tires for around five hundred dollars before your time is up.

I don't even want to think about car-wash money, wax jobs, detailing, dash mats, window tinting or window screens, gasoline, fan belts, water hoses, air-conditioning recharges, tire balancing, shock absorbers, struts, thermostat replacement, and bumper stickers that say, "My other car is a Rolls Royce."

You can see that the purchase of one piece of stuff seems innocent at first, but it will drain your dollars away as fast as you can make them. If you don't believe me, check the balance on your bank account. See what I mean?

We will not get into a discussion here of all the other stuff you could buy. There are tens of thousands of things in the world that someone is trying to sell you. It is their contention that if you will buy that piece of stuff you will be happy. You will never see a car, beer, soda pop or a hemorrhoid commercial that will claim you will be worse off for buying their product. They are all going to tell you how much better you are going to feel after driving, drinking, or applying their product to wherever you are going to drive, drink, or apply it. Isn't stuff wonderful?

Every time you spend a dollar of your money it is gone. You have taken a dollar of your money and given it to someone else. Let me tell you what happens after you give your money to the other person. Once you give it to the car dealer, bartender, vending machine, salesperson or store owner, you must give someone else more of your money to take care of the stuff you bought or to haul away your stuff's packaging container. Some stuff has to be insured. Then, when your stuff wear out, you will have it hauled away to the dump, and directly or indirectly, your money will pay for that, too.

After you buy some stuff, you will plug it into an outlet that takes your money to pay the electric bill. All of your stuff is going to break, wear out, become outdated, or get stolen after you get it. You will buy some stuff you will never use. The more stuff you own, the more stuff you have to replace when it does break, wear out or become outdated. Landfills are full of the stuff we thought we wanted.

The stuff you never use you will give away to Goodwill for a tax deduction. Let's say you donate a pair of old shoes, a shirt, a pair of pants and a belt that originally cost you one hundred fifty dollars. The fair market value is now thirteen dollars. You get one dollar back on your income tax return.

It takes money to buy stuff.

It takes money to maintain stuff.

It takes money to own stuff.

It takes money to insure stuff.

It takes money to dispose of stuff.

It takes money to replace stuff.

STUFF COSTS MONEY...

Obviously, the less stuff you own, the less stuff you have that will wear out, get broken, become outdated, get stolen, or never get used. This means you will have less stuff to repair, replace, insure, maintain, and less stuff you will have to haul away. Some of you are paying money to store stuff you are not using.

Get rid of some of your stuff, and you will save enough of your money to pay for several dates, or maybe even all your dates. Be honest with yourself on which items you can get rid of. You will find that the more stuff you rid yourself of, the more freedom you will have. A general rule is this: if you have not used it within the last year, get rid of it.

Make this your rule from this point on. It is your money. If you are going to give it to someone else, make sure it is worth it. Not only should it be worth it to give them your money for the item, it should be worth it to maintain, insure, repair, replace and haul away the item with your money. It should be worth owning the item, or it will own you.

Time with You Is What She Wants

My last word on this subject is an admonition. When something breaks, wears out, or you find you do not use it and you get rid of it, do not replace it. This alone will save a lot of your money. An old adage, "If it isn't broke, don't fix it," can be coupled with, "If it is broke, don't fix it, and don't replace it." Keep your money.

Your wife is one thing that money cannot buy. Many men have tried. Many men have lost their wives while trying to work hard and long and by giving her in dollars and stuff what their labors have earned. This is good if your time and presence is part of the gifts and money. If you send the stuff only, you will lose her. If you spend too much time away from her trying to get her more stuff, you will return home one day with more stuff and find she is gone with the "stuff" she already had.

Time with you is what she wants. Use your time wisely. Divide it between home and work in a balanced manner. Yes, you need to make a living and put a roof over your head, food on the table and clothes on your back and those in your family. These things are needs. Never confuse everything else in life with need. Everything else is wants. You don't need them.

Spend your extra money on your family, but don't substitute extra money for time with family. I promise you, in your later life, you will not regret the time you spent with family. It is all too common for men to look back when they are old and feel remorse for the missed opportunities they could have had with family.

In our house, above our bed is a large picture of the Neuschwanstein Castle. This is the castle used as a model for the castle at Disneyland. The picture above the bed is of the real castle in Germany, not the one at Disneyland. The real castle is several times larger than the one at Disneyland and sits in the forested countryside among beautiful snowcapped mountains. It is above our bed as a reminder of the trip my wife and I took to that part of the world. It is also there because it is my wife's dream house. I keep telling her someday I will either buy the castle for her or I will build one that looks just like it. Every princess needs a dream. Every knight needs an honorable goal. This castle fulfills both needs for my wife and me. She knows that if I could give it to her, I would. Who knows, someday I may.

The part of the dream that did come true was the trip to see the castle in Germany. That took five years of planning and saving. While in the area, we visited Austria and France to see other castles. In the Bavarian part of Germany and parts of Austria, we saw the areas where they filmed the movie *The Sound of Music*. It is beautiful country with breathtaking scenery. If you ever get a chance to go, do it. You most definitely will not regret it.

Decide How You Want to Travel

When you travel, you have to make a decision: to go cheap or go first class. That decision is yours alone. When we took our train trip from Germany to France, we decided to save money and not get a sleeper car. We thought we could tough it out for one night since we were going to have a nice hotel to sleep in the next night.

When night comes on the train, everyone gets comfortable. That means they take off their shoes and stretch out. We were in another country and unfamiliar with their ways. We had people sitting across from us putting their "stinky feet" up beside us as they stretched out to sleep. It was awful, to say the least. We will not get into the decibel level of the people who snored. A nice private berth in a sleeper car would have been so much more pleasant. You must decide whether or where to cut corners when you go on trips. Try to talk to those who have already been there and get their advice. My brother-in-law tried to warn us about the train. I should have listened.

My point in telling you about this trip is to get you to realize that your memories can never be taken from you. Stuff can. You come into this world with no stuff. You will leave this world with no stuff. You will have your memories firmly implanted in your mind as you leave. How many times have you heard someone say, "I thought I was going to die, and my whole life flashed before my eyes." That literally happens. Read about people who have had near-death experiences. They have their memories. So will you.

In our living room we have a miniature Eiffel tower in a curio cabinet. On our bookshelf we have a book purchased at the Louvre Museum. Above our bed we have the picture of the Neuschwanstein Castle. In our dining room we have a cuckoo clock we bought in Germany.

In photo albums we have pictures of this and other trips we have taken. On a wall in our family room we have a mounted, trophy King Salmon from our Alaska trip. On the same wall we have trophies we won together from Bass fishing tournaments. In another room is a picture of Alcatraz—a memento from a trip we took to San Francisco. By our bathtub are shells—some picked up on the beach during various trips to the ocean along the California coast. In our living room is an old milk can we picked up at an antique store in an old town in Arkansas. The family room has a carved coconut bowl from our Hawaii trip and an Ulu knife from our Alaska trip. My wife has a wood-carving the shape of Texas near the sink in the kitchen with short strands of various kinds of barbed wire used by ranchers in that state.

Our house is a museum of memories—memories created together. Every room has reminders of things we have done together. My wife is our decorator. She displays all these things for our guests to see. Do you think they bring her joy? You better believe it! We have our memories. What are your memories? Create some new ones. If you can afford to go first class, do it.

There is an interesting side note to money and dating. On question #46 in the questionnaires I circulated, I asked the

wives to list presents their husbands gave them other than for
Christmas, anniversary, birthday, and Mothers' day. Question
#47 asked the wives to list their last three anniversary gifts.
Question #48 asked them to list their three favorite gifts they
received for Mothers' Day. Finally, in question #49, I asked
them to list their three favorite birthday gifts.

The answers were fascinating. Half did not list any gifts.
They could not remember what the gifts were. I had many
answers that said "Can't remember" or "Don't remember." The
wives received gifts, but just could not remember what they
received. Most of the gifts remembered were flowers, dinners
out, jewelry, clothes, appliances, electronics, perfume, books,
CDs and trips out of town.

Several wrote comments like, "It's not the gifts, but the
'intent' that is important." Another said, "Laughter, joy, hope."
Another wrote, "A letter that my son and husband wrote."
The same woman once received "a hand picked-flower."
One woman wrote, "A special day with no responsibilities or
mothering. He cooked all the meals and supervised cleanup."
I am assuming he supervised the children, and not her, on the
cleanup. Still another wife said, "Time for myself without kids
or work, dinner out—he arranges the baby sitter—we don't do
high dollar gifts." The same woman said, "I don't have to do
anything all day."

A wife reported that she got "a thirty-second spot on the
radio with him and the kids, followed by a favorite song dedication." Another wife said, "A day to myself, he took kids away
all day! WOW!" Once this wife's husband "washed and vacu-
umed my car for me." Still another woman said, "Not having
to cook dinner."

The dates spent together were "two days spent alone at a
bed and breakfast and shopping" (with her husband). One wife
said, "Weekend in Scottsdale, hotel, meals, shopping in historic

shop area and art museums." Another wife said, "He provides me with all my possessions." Following this theme, a wife said, "Just spending time with the kids and me. Helping me with chores around the house!!"

The only negative comment I had was from a woman who said, "Diamond ring for the dates, anniversaries, birthdays he's missed." Remember what I said about money and dating? When they cannot have you, they need money or gifts that cost money. The question is, how long will your wife accept the gifts and put up with you not being around before she decides to just take the gifts and dump you? You can see from these answers that the wives' favorite gifts are you and your time.

Giving a gift is important. The best gifts are those when you give of yourself and your time. The second best gifts are where you surprise them. The least remembered gift is a thing. Wives do not remember the "thing" gifts half the time, but they forever remember the gifts of time and self.

10

Correcting Some Illusions About Dating

My competitors sometimes do as much for me as do my friends. My friends are too polite to point out my weaknesses, but my competitors go to great expense to advertise them.

My competitors are efficient, diligent, and attentive. They make me continually search for ways to improve my services.

My competitors would take my business away from me if they could. This keeps me alert to hold what I have, and to get and create even more.

My competitors prevent me from becoming lazy, incompetent, and careless. I need the discipline they enforce upon me.

My competitors deserve my highest praise. I salute them. They have been good to me.

—Unknown

How many marriages have ended because there was a male competing for some other man's wife? A soft word here, a gentle touch there, and listening and smiling when she is talking—all have their effect on a woman. When paying some attention to her, other males can be "efficient, diligent and attentive." Other males will "point out your weaknesses," if not by word, then by example. Other males would "take your business away" from you if they could.

Because there are other males out there in the world, it should keep you "alert to hold what you have." They should prevent you from "becoming lazy, incompetent and careless." If you think it cannot happen to you, talk to some formerly married males who now find themselves divorced. Better yet, talk to the wives of those divorced men and ask them what happened. I think you would get closer to the truth by talking to the women. The ex-husbands will be posturing, as males do. They will tell you it was "her fault." We all know a male can never be wrong. Right?

While researching this book, I was amazed at all the illusions I heard from men and women about dating inside marriage. The biggest illusion was that dating inside marriage does not or should not exist. Several people told me that dating is for "young people" and for "getting to know each other." Once you are married, there is no longer a need for dating.

Let me assure you, dating inside marriage does exist. I know dozens of married couples that date regularly. Whether dating should exist inside marriage is not even a close call; of course it should.

You are as young or as old as you feel. Dating is not only for "young people," it's for all people. As for the illusion that dating is for two people to "get to know each other," I have one question: What husband is there that can say he knows and understands his wife fully? I know the answer already, and it means you still need to date your wife so you can get to know her.

Illusion: There is No Need for Dating after Marriage

This next question was asked of Miss Piggy, of Muppet fame.

What should a woman do if a man stands her up on a date?

"If the man is genuinely apologetic, I would let him off with a large bunch of flowers, an expensive present, and a lavish make-up dinner. On the other hand, if he treats it in an offhand manner, he is obviously the kind of person who is not going to knock himself out for you, and you should do it for him."

—*Miss Piggy, Miss Piggy's Guide to Life*
(As Told to Henry Beard)

After twenty years as a police officer, I never advocate violence to settle anything. Miss Piggy is a fictitious character, but shares the same feelings of many women who are married. They do feel like "knocking him out" when he becomes a couch potato.

As for a need for dating, I have a simple response. Ask your wife if she feels there is a need for dating. In my surveys, I asked the question, "Would you like to have a date a week with your husband?" The response was resoundingly "yes." Over ninety-five percent answered positively.

The alarming responses were those where the wife answered "no." On one survey, the wife answered that she would not like to date her husband every week because she does not love him. She said she did not even like him and was only staying with him until the kids were grown. She said they had already discussed this and both agreed to stay together for now. A second woman who answered "no" also stated she did not love her husband. She said she liked him but did not love him.

Still another woman said her husband complains about everything and only calls her from work when he wants something, never to check on her or tell her he loves her. He also spends money on himself but not on her, and she states he is inconsiderate and disrespectful. This wife also said that she had a stale marriage and there was no romance in it. I think I can see why she did not want a date a week.

I think I can say, after reading these surveys, that your wife wants to date you. The exception is, if she does not love you any more. If you are a bore or a jerk, there's hope. You can become a better husband if you will open yourself to advice and correct a few things in your personality. Just assume, for a moment, that maybe you can improve—then try it and see what happens.

If your wife no longer loves you, it is time you find out why. I'll bet it's because you are not dating. Such was the case with the two women who answered that they no longer loved their husbands. Neither of them dates their husband now, and past dating habits are equal to their current dating habits. All the women who answered they wanted a date a week with their husbands already do some dating, and they want more.

Favorite Memories Shared with Husbands

Question #70 on the survey asked the wives to list their three favorite memories with their husbands. Here are some of their answers:

- Coaching me through labor
- Concerts
- When he puts my feelings first
- Fourth of July
- Supper on engagement in Paris
- When I met him
- Vacations with children
- Time alone
- The first "I love you"
- Our cruise
- Walking a sick baby for hours
- Our first date
- Taking care of our children
- Our marriage retreat

- Purchase of our home
- Fancy dinners out
- Shaving with our sons
- Hearing his voice
- Our first night of intimacy
- Special vacations
- Trip by bicycle around the USA
- When he tells me how beautiful I am
- When our son made Eagle Scout rank
- When he helps with my elderly frail mother
- Honeymoon (Many answered this way)
- Going to school plays to see our children
- Going to the Hilton for a week together
- Just the two of us in our first apartment
- Our wedding day (Dozens answered this way)
- Seeing him each day after we have been apart
- Taking care of me when I was pregnant
- The birth of our children (Dozens answered this way)
- The children on our first family trip
- Trip to Hawaii (and other destinations)
- Trying to braid our daughter's hair
- When he agreed to get counseling to save our marriage
- When he follows me around, hugging and kissing me
- When he hugs and talks to the children
- When he expresses love and gratitude for me
- When I told him we were going to have a baby
- When he joked around while watching television in bed
- When I came home from work and he had cleaned the entire house
- When I had our third child, I woke in the night and he was there, asleep in a chair
- When he asked me to marry him (Dozens answered this way)

• The time he left a love note on my pillow when he left on a business trip

Illusion: There Is No Room for Improvement

On his deathbed, a husband made his wife promise to buy a double grave in the cemetery and put two tombstones side by side. He then told his wife he wanted the inscription "Follow me," on his tombstone so every time she would come to visit, she would remember him and remain faithful to their relationship.

He died, and she prepared his tombstone with the inscription "Follow me." But on her tombstone she had the engraver etch these words: "To follow thee I'm not content, until I know which way you went."

Another question in our survey was, "Is there room for improvement in dating habits with your husband?" Again, the answers were ninety-five percent "yes," but the exceptions offered hope. The "no" answers were telling.

One woman said there was no room for improvement and stated, "My work is my life, and our life together is one long date." She also said, "Our whole life is a date." Finally, she said, "Every day is a date." She lists her age group as 41-50 and his as 61-70. They are both confined to wheelchairs. I agree there is no need for improvement for this lucky couple.

Three other surveys sent back to me said they needed no improvement in their dating habits. They listed dozens of dates they had been on with their husbands. They mentioned dates to Germany, France, Mexico, Hawaii, going to the opera, fishing, dancing, Las Vegas, hunting, dinner, movies, horseback riding, Bahamas, pizza, Catalina, listening to music, sitting on the front porch, scuba diving, Grand Ol' Opry, Jamaica, Australia, New Zealand, quiet evenings alone, Grand Canyon, National Parks, amusement parks, boat races, plays, zoos, symphony, swimming, picnics, watching television together, window shopping, playing scrabble, San Diego, hot air balloon festival in Albuquerque, concerts, car races, resort hotels, a weekend in a cabin, nights in a hotel, bike riding, walks, visits with friends, visits with family, Yellowstone, cruises, Tahiti, renting a limousine, ice skating, watching airplanes take off at the airport, watching fireworks on Fourth of July, Disneyland, etc.

I can see why there is no room for improvement in their dating habits. You will notice that about a third of these dates are very expensive, a third are moderately expensive, and the other third are not expensive at all. These couples have a good balance to their dating.

Include Your Wife in Things You Now Do Alone

One way you can improve your dating habits is to include your wife in things you now do alone. Survey Question #75 asked, *"What does your husband do alone now that you wish he would do with you?"*

Most women left this blank. Some wrote, "nothing," and a few wrote they understood his need to do something on his own. In my personal interviews, I found the same theme on this question. Wives understand if you need to do your "guy thing," but if you can include your wife, she would like it. A wife said she lives in a house full of guys (she has several sons). She said she feels left out at times because "they go and I stay." Ask your wife what she would like to do.

Some of the answers received to Survey Question #75, *"What does your husband do alone now that you wish he would do with you?"* include:
- Take me along on side jobs
- Fish
- Ride his . . . motorcycle
- Exercise
- I wish he would fly more often

- Sailing
- Work on his computer
- Bicycling
- More lunches together
- Tennis
- Everything he does, I like to be included
- Golf (Many women wanted to do this)

So, husbands, take her along once in a while when you "do your thing." Create a bond during these times together. Have fun together. If you do not feel guilty about your dating habits with your wife, maybe you have a good relationship already.

Illusion: We Have to Watch the Children

We cannot date because we have children at home is a dangerous illusion. When you have children at home, it is even more imperative that you date your wife. There are dozens of reasons you need to date your wife when you have children and are raising your family.

First, you are a role model. You are the role model as far as your children are concerned. Parents and other adults are also role models. Charles Barkley (then a member of the Phoenix Suns) caused an uproar when he appeared in a television commercial and said, "I am not a role model." The point of the commercial was that Charles Barkley plays basketball for money, and parents, not sports stars, should be the role models. But Charles realizes that besides being paid to play basketball, he is also a role model. He may be a good or bad one, but he is a role model. Good or bad, parents are the main role models for their children.

I included a letter with the surveys I passed out while researching this book. In the letter, I said, "The best thing a man can do for his children and his marriage is to love and show love to his wife."

Because you are a role model in your home, you must be aware that your children watch your every move. You are teaching daily by doing whatever it is you do. If you treat your wife with some disrespect, your children will pick up on it very quickly.

Similarly, if you treat her as a special person, your children will learn that she truly is special. Later, they will treat their spouses as someone special. By setting the proper example in your home, you can break the trend of broken homes, mistreated wives and children, and violence in the home and community.

You can hire a baby-sitter or swap baby-sitting with other couples so you can date. There are a few all-night day care centers; find one for a couple of hours once in awhile when all else fails. Your parents or hers can sit with the children on occasion. So can your brothers or sisters, or your wife's brothers and sisters. There are also other relatives, friends and neighbors. I know you can find a way to have time for your wife. You must date if you have children in the home, for their sake and for society's sake.

Some families have started baby-sitting co-ops. Any baby-sitting done is paid for with tokens that can be redeemed for an equal number of baby-sitting hours. The more families in the co-op, the more parents are available to watch your children while you spend that important time with your wife.

If nothing else, include the children on your date. Do things that can be enjoyed together, like going to the park, horseback riding, the beach, strolling through the mall, going to a bookstore or to sporting events. While I believe marital intimacy belongs in private, it's a fine example for the children to see you holding your wife's hand or sharing a hug, even in public. Former president George Bush said, "What you do in your own house is more important than what goes on in the White House."

Illusion: Apologizing Is a Sign of Weakness

The comments of a few husbands who knew of this book while I was writing it disturbed me. One was, "If I start all this dating stuff now, she will think I am having an affair or something." Another was, "If I start dating now, I will have to apologize for all the times I didn't date." A variation of the last thought was, "If I start dating now, it will show how much I ignored her in the past, and she will resent it."

Let's take that first comment about having an affair. If you are making time for the other woman and not for your wife, that is when she is going to be suspicious. When you call and say, "Honey I'm working late," her suspicion will heighten. When you call and say, "Honey, I'm coming home from work so we can be together," she may wonder if you have suddenly become ill. However, I don't think she will accuse you of having an affair. She is going to be one happy camper to have you coming home to pay some attention to her.

The second comment, about apologizing, is totally incorrect. You will not have to apologize for the times you have not dated your wife, but you should. If you have ignored your wife or treated her badly, it is a good idea to apologize.

Apologizing is not a sign of weakness; it is a sign of strength. When you apologize, your wife will think highly of you. It takes a really strong man to acknowledge being wrong. Just sit down with her some evening and tell her you have not been doing as well in your role as a husband as you would like. Then commit to do better. Watch her reaction. It'll make the apology worthwhile.

Remember the movie *Love Story,* with Ryan O'Neal and Ali McGraw? There is one line in that movie that at first seemed really loving to me, but after I thought about it awhile, I realized how badly it turned out. The line was, "Love is never having to say you're sorry."

At first, a person would think, yes, that is the way it should be. When a couple loves and understands each other, they should know when the other person is sorry, and an apology would never have to be spoken. I am here to tell you that an apology needs verbalization. Never assume she knows you are sorry, and never assume you can skip the apology and everything will turn out all right. You must say the words.

Besides apologizing to our wives, we should be aware of wrongs committed against our children and apologize to them. One day I was going to take my son out to lunch so we could have time together. I do this with each of my children. I am hypoglycemic, and when I have not had anything to eat for a few hours, I get headaches and other physical symptoms that cause me to be irritable. While I was waiting for my son to finish mowing the yard so we could go, I began to have one of my "attacks."

When my son finished the yard, I was well on my way to a good headache. I raised my voice and wanted to know when we were going to go. He immediately got ready to go, and we went to lunch. Once we seated ourselves at the restaurant, I told him I was sorry for acting the way I did. He forgave me and we had a good talk about things that were going on in his life that were important to him. Had I not apologized, it would have been a miserable lunch.

When you apologize, there are certain things for which you need to be aware. You cannot just go to her and say, "I'm sorry," give her a hug, walk away and assume she knows what you are talking about. You need to be specific. Let's say you just came home from work and your wife says, "Mom wants us to come over tonight for a couple of hours." You had a difficult experience as you drove home from work, so you vent your frustration, saying, "Your mother is such a bore. I don't want to go."

It is now time for an apology. Say, "I am sorry I called your mother a bore." That is more specific than "I am sorry for what I said about your mother."

The next step in apologizing is to tell her why you acted that way. "I had a hard day at work, and on the way home a guy cut me off in traffic. I was so full of frustration I exploded."

At this point you apologize again, telling her you are sorry for the pain you caused her personally. That is different from the first apology where you were only remorseful for the words you spoke. Now you are remorseful for the discomfort the words caused her.

Next you tell her you love her. Then you promise to never do it again. Now you have to make it up to her. You do not have to go overboard here like buying her a fur coat or a car, but you do need to do something. Maybe take her out for a soda or dessert. You can do this on the way to or from her mother's house. But what is important is that you need to talk to her now. Do not let this opportunity go by without expressing your love and appreciation for her.

The most important part of apologizing is changing your ways. Make a commitment to her and to yourself that the thing you did or said will never happen again, and then stick to that promise. This is the way to create trust in a marriage. If you promise never to call her mother a name again, you had better stick to that promise.

It is important that you understand that apologizing is a sign of personal strength. The false illusion some people cling to is that apologizing makes you weak. Don't fall for this illusion. Benjamin Franklin acknowledged, "None but the well-bred man knows how to confess a fault, or acknowledge himself in error." Apologize when appropriate.

Illusion: Dating Costs Lots of Money

That brings me to another of the illusions about dating. It always costs lots of money. My response to that is it does not have to cost money. There are enough dates that cost no money listed in this book that you could date for a year without spending anything. You will only need to put gas in your car and grab something out of the refrigerator for your food if you want to. I hope with a little thought on your part, you can come up with other dates that cost no money.

Here are a few answers to question #34 in the survey, *"List four dates you enjoyed having with your husband that cost no money."*
- Viewing Christmas decorations
- Window shopping
- Target shooting
- Watching fireworks
- Photographing wild flowers
- Exploring cemeteries
- Visiting art museums
- Drives in the country
- Fishing (digging your worms)
- Making love
- Barbecue in the back yard
- Going to church
- Playing Ping-Pong
- Riding Quads
- Watching the sun rise
- Hiking
- Movie night at home
- Playing darts
- Playing on a playground

- Visiting the library
- Cruising downtown at night
- Tennis
- Visiting family or friends
- Listening to music
- Visiting the elderly or sick
- Basketball
- Camping in the back yard
- Hunting
- Browsing a book store
- Staying home alone
- Putting together jigsaw puzzles
- Bike riding
- Feeding the ducks and geese
- Taking a walk
- Evenings in front of the fireplace
- Going to special events at other churches
- Sitting on the porch in the evening
- Picnic using candles and making S'mores
- Watching television together snuggled on the couch
- Driving around looking at houses and nice yards
- Having talks and really listening to each other
- Watching planes land and take off at the airport
- Bluebonnet looking (looking for Bluebonnet flowers in Texas in the spring)
- Going to dog shows where my husband shows his champion German shepherd

And you might get ideas with the answers to question #36: "List five dates you have enjoyed with your husband that only cost one to twenty dollars."

- Breakfast by a campfire
- Eating at fast food place
- Tennis and movie afterward

- Video game arcade
- Going to the flea market
- Water slide
- Lunch together
- Visiting the zoo
- Going to a restaurant
- Ice cream cafe
- A symphony on a river bank
- Bowling
- Visiting an antique shop
- Hot rod races
- Going to get hot chocolate
- Target practicing
- Muscle car shows
- Horseback riding
- Watching videos at home
- Home Shows
- Going to a play or concert
- Float trip on a river
- Going to a golf driving range
- Miniature golf
- Going to a comedy club
- Going to the State Fair
- Sight-seeing
- Ice skating show
- Gin games in bed with pizza
- Movie
- Driving to another city for dinner
- Dancing
- Each bought a book at a book store
- Bought flowers for me and took a drive
- Renting a telescope—going went to the desert to look at the stars

- Bought a CD and went home to listen to it
- Scouting for a hunting trip for elk, deer, turkey, etc.
- Going to mashed potato/lizard cook off (A Texas wife)
- Football, basketball or baseball games at High Schools
  or Universities

Dating is simply spending time with your wife, and spending it alone with her when possible. There is no substitute for time spent together!

11

Overcoming Excuses for Not Dating

*It is not marriage that fails, it is people that fail.
All that marriage does is to show people up.*
— *Harry Emerson Fosdick*

Where there is a problem, there is a solution. Always! We just have not discovered all the solutions yet. Man invented the wheel to help carry and move burdens. Several thousand years later, he invented the automobile to carry those same burdens and get from one place to another faster. He then invented the airplane to move still faster. Man has invented microwave ovens, electric can openers, garage door openers, computers, fax machines, light bulbs, and hundreds of other items. All of this in the name of saving labor and time.

You no longer prepare fields for planting with mules pulling plows. I know you don't hitch up the buggy to the horses and drive for an hour into town to buy from the merchant. You don't have to chop wood to put in the oven to cook dinner or to put on the fireplace to keep warm in winter. The lanterns don't need filling with kerosene for light. You just flip a switch. You're a fortunate person living in a fortunate nation.

109

I pose the question, "What is happening with all the time you are saving?" It is time to use time—to spend time—with your wife.

You will find many solutions, but not all solutions, to your dating habits in this book. Use the ideas you find, and let them be a springboard to help you think of other solutions. Just do something!

There are definite steps to solving problems. First, identify the problem. Second, make a list of possible solutions. They can be simple or crazy, complex or sublime. Third, enact the best solution from the list. Fourth, if that solution fails, try another solution from the list. If all solutions fail, create new solutions.

There were a few excuses given to the question on the survey when asked, "What excuses does your husband give for not going out on dates?" To be fair, I also asked the wives, "What excuses do you give for not going out on dates?" The answers were the same and showed up repeatedly. It seems every man and woman gives the same excuses.

Excuse: I'm Too Tired

Grandpa sat on the porch with me, reflecting on the "good old days." Speaking of Grandma, he stated, "I wonder what happened to the old-fashioned girl who used to faint when I kissed her?"

The screen door creaked, and Grandma stepped out with a tray of lemonade. She gave him a look and asked, "What ever happened to the old-fashioned guy who could kiss me and make me faint?"

Being too tired was the number one excuse on the survey. The survey asked for the husband's occupation. After reading the occupations, I wondered how so many men got away with this excuse for not dating. I realize that some jobs are physically demanding, and others are mentally or emotionally draining.

Think about the message you are sending your wife when you give this excuse. An electrician, plumber, or air-conditioning technician says he is too tired to go out. He is saying, "I can splice wires, install a sink, or run duct work, but I'm too tired to drive you to dinner and eat."

A fire fighter, police officer, or ambulance driver says he is too tired. "Honey, I can treat accident victims, fight with prisoners, drive to the hospital, but I'm just too tired to drive you to get ice cream."

A roofer, carpenter, or mason tells his wife he can nail shingles, cut studs or lay bricks in one-hundred-degree temperatures for eight hours, but he is too tired to drive to a movie theater and sit in an air-conditioned building to watch a movie.

A doctor, lawyer, or business owner says he can treat clients, make phone calls, dictate orders to employees, but says he is too tired to take a walk around the block after sitting in an office all day.

I think all these males failed the truth test. "I'm tired," sounds good to you as it rolls off your lips, but it does not wash. Your wives hear your words, but what they really hear is, "My wife doesn't mean as much to me as watching the game on television." The amount of energy required for most dates is nothing compared to what you do for a living. You have the energy for your boss and your wife, too—you just need to readjust your priorities.

Excuse: I'm Too Busy

"I don't have the time right now" usually means, "I will not make the time right now." This excuse goes over really well with your wife. About five minutes after you tell her this, you are in front of the television with the remote control. I guess you think somehow you are invisible when you jump in the recliner, and that she really cannot see you sitting there "being busy!"

Sometimes, you really may be busy. You may have an office in your home and you may have to do some work in that office. If you are failing to make time for your wife, and if this is an everyday occurrence, it's time to consider another occupation. There simply must be a time each day you can take a few minutes and talk to your wife. If you can talk on the phone, you can talk to your wife. Let the recorder answer the next call. Call them back in twenty minutes and talk to your wife for that twenty minutes. Once a week, you can even let the calls go for a couple of hours.

If you were going to be busy doing chores around the house like mowing the yard, go ahead and mow the yard while the sun shines. Afterward, take her out to dinner, even if it's only to Taco Bell. You have to eat sometime, don't you?

I have one last word about time. Each hour, you have sixty minutes. Time—each day you have all there is. Use some for your wife.

Excuse: I Don't Feel Well

"I don't feel well" is close to "I'm tired." Not feeling well happens to everyone occasionally. But if you do not feel well three out of seven nights, something is wrong, and you had better see a doctor. This excuse, just like the "I'm tired" excuse, does not hold much water when used repeatedly. What you are doing is sending her the message, "I don't feel well enough to sit on the porch and watch the sunset with you, but I feel well enough to sit here and watch television and read the paper." How do you think she feels when you constantly use this excuse and then expend energy on yourself while telling her you have no energy for her?

Remember when your children did not want to go to school, and they would use the old "I don't feel well" excuse? The only way you could get your children feeling better and back in school was to make them stay in bed all day. You didn't allow them to play with their friends. They couldn't watch television. They couldn't play games. They were really miserable that day, and school looked good the next morning.

Excuse: We Have Children

Don't use your children as an excuse for not spending time with your wife. The excuse of not having a baby-sitter should be unacceptable in most cases.

I heard one husband tell his wife he could not go out with her because he wanted to spend time with the children. But then he did not spend time with the children. He went off golfing with his friends.

I would hope that this excuse of having to watch the children is never used again. Like I said in the previous chapter, take the kids with you if you have to. Swap baby-sitting tonight with another couple for tomorrow night. Schedule it ahead of time. You watch their kids Friday night and they watch yours Saturday night. It becomes a mutually beneficial situation for each couple.

Excuse: We Don't Have Any Money

When I was attending a University I was just newly married and money was scarce. We both had part-time jobs just to survive. One day, my wife came home from work wearing a new dress. She said, "Now, don't get mad, just tell me if you like it."

It did look nice, but you have to be firm with a new wife. I said, "Honey, why did you buy that? You know we don't have any money." She started to cry and said, "I don't know, the Devil must have tempted me."

I said, "You have heard in church that when the Devil tempts you, you should say, 'Get thee behind me, Satan.'"

She wailed, "I did."

"Well, what did he say?" I asked. My wife replied, "The Devil told me, 'Boy it sure looks good from the back.'"

You don't need a bulging wallet for dating. When using this excuse, you are really saying, "I failed to plan." It's true; some things you do on dates will cost money. The main thing to remember here is that you need to make sure the money goes for the two of you. It does not go just for you or just for her. The money is for things you can do together. There is no sub-stitute for time spent together.

If you want to go on a date next weekend that costs money, now is the time to start gathering the money for that date. If you wait until Friday night and then wonder where you are going to get the money, you will not have enough.

Planning now for those dates that are going to cost money is a good idea. You may not know where you are going to go, or exactly how much it is going to cost three weeks from now. You do know you are going to go on a date sometime that is going to cost money. Gather the money today and every day so you will have it. The best way to have money for dates is not to spend money on other things. The question each week is not, "Do you want to go out this week?" The proper questions are, "Where do you want to go this week? What is it that you want to do this week?"

Excuse: I Don't Want to Do That

Marvin J. Ashton once said, "Striving can be more impor-tant than arriving. If you are striving for excellence—if you are trying your best day by day with the wisest use of your time and energy to reach realistic goals—you are a success."

I hope this book solves this excuse. The excuse is now such a weak one that it is abolished from the excuse bank forever. If you do not want to do 80 percent of the things in this book, it is all right. However, if you do not want to do anything listed in this book, there is cause for concern.

I hope that you can use at least 10 or 20 percent of these ideas. As you read these things, other ideas should pop into your head and you can use those ideas. As you read, write down your ideas right in the white space in the book.

Excuse: I'm Going Out with the Guys

Going out with the guys is fine. However, if you are not matching that with a night out with your wife each week, you may have a problem. You may not see the problem, or you may not admit the problem, but you may have one. It's just a matter of time until the problem becomes evident. When it does become evident, it will explode onto the scene.

A wife will only put up with this "going out with the guys" behavior so long. It may be a few weeks, months, or even years before she puts her foot down. When the shoe drops, it is going to be an extra-large boot with a steel toe.

In talking to women about this excuse, I learned two things. The first is that a woman understands when a man needs to be with the guys. They understand because they like being with the ladies. Both sexes have this phenomenon in common. Both need interactions with the opposite sex, and both need to have some friendship time with people of their same gender.

Sometimes the contact we have with people of our same gender at work or other social gatherings is all that is necessary. Other times, a man may feel he needs an afternoon to golf with the guys. Maybe he wants to go fishing with the guys, or possibly work on the car with the guys. Similarly, the wife needs her time with Sally, Sue and Sarah. Because she needs this time, she understands your need to be with your male friends.

The other thing I learned on this subject is important for your physical and mental welfare. Although your wife understands this need to spend time with your friends, it should not exceed the time you spend with her. If you spend three hours with Bill working on the car, you need three hours of time for your wife.

Magnification Improves Attitude

"Am I doing what is required of me?" That one question defines the difference between a good result and a poor result. Many males do what is required of them and no more. A few do less than required. The rest do more than is required. The only thing separating the top ten percent from the bottom 10 percent is not the other 80 percent, but their attitudes.

The word "magnify" describes the 10 percent that does more than required. To me, "magnify" means to make more exciting, to intensify, to heighten, to increase or amplify. Imagine the difference between a date with your wife and a magnified date with your wife.

You ask your wife if she wants to go to dinner. When she says yes, you tell her where you are going and when. When the time arrives, you put your shoes on, wander out to the car, and honk the horn and yell, "Let's go." When you arrive at Taco Bell you get out of the car and walk briskly to the door and through it so you can get in line. You are hungry. You turn around to see where she is and see her dodging a car racing for the drive-thru window. Three people have arrived in line behind you. You ask her what she wants and then tell her all you have on you is three dollars so she'll have to help pay. During your meal you talk about your problems and cut her off when she tries to talk. The Pepsi is a little stronger than normal and you belch a couple of times and comment in a loud voice for all to hear, "Good Pepsi." Romantic, huh?

Compare that with the following: for a magnified dinner date you could write an invitation on your computer, printing it out on a color printer. The invitation names the time and place. Make reservations at a nice restaurant where she will want to dress up (we're not talking McDonald's here). Don't forget the R.S.V.P. at the bottom of the note or card.

Before the time arrives, wash the car and polish your shoes. Put on your dress shirt and tie and perhaps retrieve the corsage from the refrigerator. Pin it on her and help her on with her wrap or jacket and walk her to the car. Open the door for her, and when you arrive at the restaurant, don't forget to open the door for her again. Walk from the parking lot holding hands or with your arm around her waist, and open the door into the restaurant for her.

Hold hands across the table while waiting for your food to arrive. Look into her eyes when she talks to you. Listen to her, smile at her. Speak softly when it's your turn to speak. Tell her you love her and wish you could treat her like this every night because she deserves it. Mean what you say, and act like you mean it.

This is a magnified date. What will the end result be when you get home? Use your imagination here. My imagination tells me this date will turn out very well. Because of magnification, the anticipation and expectations were enhanced for both parties involved in the second date. Thus, their attitudes improved significantly. Magnification improves attitude.

However, when the thought of magnification of the date first crossed your mind, your attitude improved. It is a matter of what came first, the chicken or the egg. I submit that it does not matter. Improve your attitude and you will magnify your dates. Or, you can magnify your dates and improve your attitude.

I cannot be convinced that attitude plays no part in life. To picture the negative, one must first picture the positive, and then erase it. There are many examples of men who have emerged from the slums to attain greatness due to their attitudes. Many people have overcome disabilities heroically and attained magnificence by employing positive attitudes. People from less than ordinary backgrounds have become famous by turning around their lives, using improved attitudes. People considered failures have triumphed after a time by changing their attitudes.

I am not so naive to suggest that a simple attitude change can overcome everything in life. There are other parts in the equation that entail preparation, dedication and work. Attitude is simply the first step or the foundation.

Attitude without Action Is Useless

Attitude without action is useless. It takes attitude and action to cause the kind of relationship you would like to have with your wife. When you have a poor attitude, you will fail. If you procrastinate your actions, you fail. At the point you come to realize that it takes a good attitude coupled with preparation and action to succeed, you will succeed.

The only thing stopping you from dating your wife is you. It may be because of your attitude. If it is your attitude, change it. I know this is difficult, but all things in life worth doing are usually difficult to accomplish. It may be that your failure to act has stopped you. If so, get up and act. If you fail once, try again. Never, ever, give up.

If you believe in a higher power, God, Allah, or anyone else, ask Him to help you be a better husband. Commit to yourself and your wife to become a better husband. Believe it, prepare for it, and then act upon it!

12

What Wives Like To Do

A woman can stand anything but being forgotten, not being needed.

—*Mary Stewart Cutting*

Let's make this simple. Wives want to do just about anything on a date. During my discussions with married women, they mentioned scores and scores of things they would like to do on dates. You will find them listed elsewhere in the book.

Almost invariably, when I would ask a married woman, "What would you like to do on a date with your husband?" She would answer, "Anything." Your wife almost means it when she says, "Anything." What she cares about most is you. Where you go or what you do is secondary.

The danger here, though, lies in the fact that she may not do some things on a date. Most women do not want to go skydiving or bungee jumping. A few do not want to do almost everything on the lists. So what does a woman mean when she says, "Anything?"

What she means is this: "We do so little now, that I would be willing to do almost anything." Or, "I would be willing to do a lot to be with my husband." It also means, "I wish he would pay some attention to me."

Be Both Physically and Emotionally Available

I am not saying you ignore your wife all the time, but you do ignore her or take her for granted at times. You don't do this intentionally. You get comfortable and slide into bad habits over time. Being physically present with your wife is not the same as being emotionally available.

If you are not giving her as much time as you are giving your male friends, it is time to re-evaluate your habits. There are good habits and bad habits. Spending more time with someone else above the time you spend with your wife is a bad habit. It is time to change. Every wife I talked with, wanted equal time. Some admitted to nagging when their husbands didn't give them their time. If you feel you are being nagged, re-evaluate the amount of time you give to your wife. After all, it was to her you promised yourself at your wedding.

The following chapters on weekly and quarterly dates, anniversaries and five-year trips have suggestions on what wives want to do and places they'd like to go on dates.

In the survey question #90: "*Date-wise, what three things is your husband doing now that you would like to see him keep doing?*" many answers came up repeatedly. "Looking nice," "grooming," and being "clean and sweet-smelling" came up several times, so it must be important.

The suggestions below came from survey questions: #91, 92 95: "*Date-wise, what three things is your husband not now doing that you would like to see him do?*"; "*Date-wise, what three things is your husband now doing that you would like to have him stop doing?*"; "*What can your husband do to help you prepare for dates?*"

What Wives Enjoy on Dates

The list comes from women who are currently successfully married. By successfully married, I mean that they said they are happy with the things their husbands do. These are the things their husbands do to make their marriages successful.

- Asking me on dates
- Telling me I look nice
- Pulling out the chair for me
- Being flexible
- Being open-minded to try new things
- Hugging me
- Talking with me about anything
- Touching
- Being helpful around the house
- Being available
- Sharing his day with me
- Opening doors
- Being energetic
- Kissing me
- Telling me he loves me
- Holding hands
- Arranging the baby-sitter
- Spontaneity
- Having time without the kids
- Laughing and joking
- Going where I want to go
- Having quiet evenings
- Budgeting time for me
- Smiling
- Showing affection in public
- Being creative
- Being well-groomed when we go out
- Asking me what I would like to do
- Acting like he enjoys being with me
- Letting me go with him on business trips
- Being enthusiastic about going out

- Going out with friends occasionally
- Being considerate of my feelings
- Sending flowers for no special reason
- Taking me to dinner so I don't have to fix it
- Arranging his time to be with me
- Taking the grandkid's on outings
- Continuing to ask even when it doesn't work out
- Sex. Sex. Sex. (This from a 71+ year-old woman with a 71+ year-old husband)

Husband Behavior Which Wives Do Not Like

There were many answers to the survey question of what wives do not care for. I let a co-worker (who is married for the second time) read this list. She kept laughing and I finally asked her why? She said it reminded her of her ex-husband (ex- being the key part) and she wanted to buy a copy of the book and send it to him with a note that says, "If you want to know what happened in our marriage, read this book."

Each of us is probably guilty of a few of these infractions. You could mark each item where you feel a little guilty. You might ask your wife to read and mark the list also. This could give you two different pictures of yourself. William Shakespeare observed, "Men's faults do seldom to themselves appear."

Wives do not like:
- Husbands who never take them on dates, or are "cheap" on dates
- Husbands who do not talk to them
- Husbands who take them for granted
- Husbands who do not say, "I love you"
- Husbands who never say "Thank you"
- Husbands who do not snuggle
- Husbands who work too much

- Husbands who watch too much television
- Husbands who do not spend time with the children
- Husbands who do not laugh or who do not make their wives laugh
- Husbands who are not sociable with their wife's friends
- Husbands who bring friends on dates
- Husbands who do not kiss them
- Husbands who fail to say, "You look good" or "You look sexy"
- Husbands who go out with their friends and not their wives
- Husbands who are "not really there" when they go out
- Husbands who give gifts to relieve guilt but don't change their behavior
- Husbands who treat other people better than their wife

13

Daily Dating Habits

Oh, the comfort, the inexpressible comfort, of feeling safe with a person, having neither to weigh thoughts, nor measure words—but pouring them all right out—just as they are—chaff and grain together—certain that a faithful hand will take and sift them—keep what is worth keeping—and with the breath of kindness blow the rest away.
—*Dinah Maria Mulock*

Make Your Love for Your Wife Visible to Others

I was listening to a friend the other day as he told this story to a group of our acquaintances. He said he was reading a book to his son and daughter as they sat on either side of him. At one point in the story he paused and his daughter suddenly asked, "Daddy, do you love Mommy?" Stunned for a moment due to the seriousness of the question, he hesitated to answer. He assumed his children knew he loved their mother. He wondered for a moment why his daughter would ask this question. Over his fears of what his daughter's response might be, he asked her, "What makes you ask, sweetheart?" She innocently replied, "Because I never see you kiss my mommy and you almost never give her hugs and you never hold hands like my friend Rachel's mommy and daddy."

This came from a child who had barely turned five years old. My friend's new awareness caused him to realize his shortcoming and his potentialities. My friend now kisses, hugs, and holds hands with his wife in front of his children. Do you think children learn by example?

My friend told his daughter that he loved her mommy very much. He told her he had not been doing all that he could to show mommy that he loved her. My friend promised to do better and has lived up to his promises.

If you have children in your house, I hope you are showing them that you love their mother. If you do not have children, I hope you are showing your wife that you love her. Try to list the things you did in the last seventy-two hours to show your wife you love her. It may be as simple as kissing her good-bye when you go off to work, or gazing into her eyes when she tells you about her day.

1 _____

_____

2 _____

_____

3 _____

_____

4 _____

_____

5_____

_____

6_____

_____

7_____

_____

8_____

_____

9_____

_____

I listed nine spaces for your responses. This is the minimum you should be doing according to the wives I interviewed. If you are doing three things per day to show your love, you are just a touch above average.

Wives feel that if a husband evidences one thing each day to show his love, he just exists. If a husband is doing three things per day, wives feel he is making an effort.

The ideal would be for you to do several things per day. This way, you are ahead in the game when it comes time to add up your score for the day or week or month. One thing you may want to do after completing a good deed is to tell your wife in a kind way that you did it. Say something like, "Honey, I washed the dishes and took out the garbage; is there anything else I can do for you?"

Let's pretend you are an average guy with an average job. You get up in the morning and step into the bathroom to do your morning chore and then you head for the shower. Next, you shave, comb your hair, install deodorant in the proper places and brush your teeth. You stop at the kitchen and get your Pop-tart, milk, and banana for breakfast. You pick up your car keys and head for the door to the garage. As you pass through the door you pause, look back at the woman you call your wife and say, "See you when I get home." The door closes, and she is left with the aftermath of your getting ready for work.

She goes in the bathroom and finds that you left the seat up again. There lies your towel on the floor and the bath mat too. Beside the sink is a can of shave cream, a razor, and some aftershave lotion. A stick of deodorant, the comb, the toothpaste, a toothbrush and floss are there, too. Beard stubble inside the sink is evident, as is the hair that fell out, which is lying all around the side of the sink where it landed after you combed it right off your head.

She finds your dirty underwear on the bedroom floor where you dropped them on the way to the shower. They are near the socks you threw down beside the bed just before you crawled between the covers last night.

As she walks into the kitchen, she spies the banana peel on the counter, along with the foil wrapper from the Pop-tart. Yes, and there sits the glass with an ounce of milk in the bottom that you did not take time to finish. The crumbs on the floor from the Pop-tart are now very routine and nothing new. She knows you are not going to eat that Pop-tart over a paper plate.

She looks out the window as you drive away and says, "I love you?" That is a question mark after the word *you*. I'll bet she just cannot wait for you to get home so she can start her cleaning chores again.

I understand why you do what you do. I am a guy, too. You leave all that stuff lying around because you know it is only a two-minute job to clean it all up. It is such a small thing, and it is not worth your time to even stop and think about it. It is such a trivial thing that surely your wife can handle it. It is such an insignificant thing that it's not worth fighting about.

There are more important and bigger things to worry about. It is beneath you to worry about a measly two-minute job. Why does your wife make such a big deal out of such an insignificant thing? These things, in your view, are insignificant, meaningless, irrelevant, trivial, inconsequential, and unimportant.

If this is true, then why don't you do them? Why leave them to your wife? I agree that they are insignificant things and not worth arguing or fighting about. Sometimes I pick up my things and put them away, sometimes I don't. Sometimes I pick up my things but don't put the other things away. Sometimes I eat over paper plates and sometimes I don't. Sometimes I do none of these things.

The point is, sometimes I do. I am willing to help. My wife knows I am willing to help. She knows sometimes I am running late or working on a project and do not have two minutes to pick up after myself. She also knows that when I do have time, I will help her. She figured out a long time ago that I am not perfect and will not become so in this life. She knows I do try and that I will continue to do so. I am not the standard in husbands. I am an example for you to exceed.

The threat in a marriage comes when the husband does not show he is willing to help sometimes. A wife will only tolerate this attitude so long. Then you are looking at retaliation—ranging from her refusal to pick up after you to nagging you about not helping. She could, if it has gone on long enough, divorce you. This will come when she gets tired and you show no signs of caring or improving.

We have talked of habits in previous chapters and that is a theme of this book. The philosopher Aristotle stated, "Men acquire a particular quality by constantly acting in a particular way." You are as you are because of your habits. If you are a good husband, it is due to conscientious habits. If you are a poor husband, it is due to inferior habits.

When you prepare yourself for a crisis by forming proper habits, you can confidently wait out any storm that may occur in your marriage. When you acquire considerate habits, you will be benevolent when you discover discord. If you form appropriate habits, you shall not fear tumult that appears at your door.

Cultivate Laughter

A good habit to cultivate in a marriage is the habit of laughter. In my survey from many wives, and in my personal interviews with wives, they mentioned laughter often. They want to be happy, and a thermometer of happiness is the number of times you laugh together. Tell her a joke every day. Listen to the radio disc jockeys or television comedians, and repeat a good joke when you hear one. Sometimes the guys at work will tell a clean one you can use and re-tell at home. Do not tell rude, crude or debasing jokes. Buy a joke book at a bookstore if you need to. Laughter in a marriage will heal many wounds and create togetherness. To become a better husband, look to your past habits and improve upon them. America's first president, George Washington, verbalized the following. "We ought not to look back unless it is to derive useful lessons from past errors, and for the purpose of profiting by dear-bought experience."

The list below will help you to take a "look back" at your past habits. It will help you "derive useful lessons from past errors." It will help you recognize some things you can do to improve yourself as a husband. It will help you form the habits that will carry you through many memorable years with your wife. Just pick two or three of these each day and do them. More than three would be better because it shows you are trying harder. As you read these and think of others, write them in the columns so you can refer to them later.

- Give her a full body massage
- Caress her
- Touch her when you talk to her
- Snuggle in bed
- Wash a load of clothes
- Dry a load of clothes
- Pick up the kids for her
- Dust for her
- Leave a flower on her pillow
- Let the dog or cat out
- Leave a love note on her pillow
- Make the bed with her
- Open building doors for her
- Read poetry to her
- Carry in the groceries
- Take out the garbage
- Hold hands in public
- Put the seat down
- Run your fingers through her hair
- Hang up your clothes
- Take a bath or shower together
- Write her a poem
- Brag about her in front of others
- Take a nap together
- Brush her hair at night before bed
- Send her a telegram

- Open the car door for her
- Bring her a cold drink
- Fill the tires in her car with air
- Vacuum the floor for her
- Wash and dry the dishes with her
- Buy her a book by her favorite author
- Buy a subscription to her favorite magazine
- Buy her a greeting card for no reason
- Take a walk around the neighborhood
- Massage her feet and/or shoulders
- Make her a dessert in the shape of a heart
- Fold a load of clothes and put them away
- Wash her car for her or have it washed
- Wash her hair for her—use lots of shampoo
- Take care of her when she is sick
- Fix something around the house
- Buy a bottle of her favorite perfume
- Buy her a card telling her you love her
- Carve your names in a tree in your yard
- Start a photo album of the two of you
- Order a T-shirt made with a message to her from you
- Sit with your wife on the couch and put your arm around her
- Buy her favorite magazine and bring it home to her
- Have a radio station dedicate her favorite song from you
- Kiss her (It takes thirty-four facial muscles to kiss)
- Take or pick up some clothes to the dry cleaners for her
- Play footsy under the table with her
- If you have a home computer with a modem, fax her a note
- Have your major anniversaries written up in the newspaper
- If you travel across ice or water or other slippery

surfaces, hold on to her
- Change the air-conditioning filters in your home
- Take her car for an oil change or change it yourself
- Tell her how happy you are that you married her
- Cool down or warm up the car before you pick her up
- Stop by a bakery and bring home her favorite pastry
- Get a blanket and cover her or share it with her on a cold day
- Encourage her to visit with her parents, especially her mother
- Wash your car before you take her out, especially clean up the inside
- While sitting near her, turn and smile at her and wink at her
- If she is going to miss it, tape her favorite T.V. show
- Run her bath water for her—remember the suds
- Take her to her doctor appointments when possible
- Order a trophy made for her engraved with "First Place Wife"
- Tell her how smart she is every chance you get
- Tell her, "If I had it to do all over, I would have married you sooner"
- Let her have time with a girlfriend when she wants it
- Understand when it's "that time of the month"
- Buy a life insurance policy to take care of her when you are gone
- Kiss her neck or bite her ear (Gently, of course)
- When she has supported you, give her recognition when talking to friends
- Make sure you have her picture in your wallet
- Visit her at work on occasion, if her boss allows it
- Stop by a store on your way home from work and buy her favorite fruit

- Go to a gift shop and buy something for her
- Do the grocery shopping sometime when she is too busy to do it
- Hire a house-cleaning service for a week or month
- Call her voice mail or answering machine and leave a loving message
- Go to a magic store and bring home a trick to show her
- Order a singing telegram delivered to her at work or at home
- When out to dinner, on an airplane, or elsewhere, let her choose her seat
- Go to the store, buy some oranges, and squeeze her some fresh juice
- Pick up your socks (Or, don't drop them on the floor in the first place)
- Be there when the baby is born (With a camera if she agrees)
- Call her from work or wherever you happen to be to tell her you love her
- Have pens or pencils engraved with her name
- Pray together before going to bed (Express in your prayer, your thanks for her and all she does for you and your family. This way you verbally show her you care)
- Buy her a gift basket of some kind (Bath lotions or sweet smelling perfumes, etc.)
- A print shop can make stationery with her name on it with a message from you
- Hug her (Many wives say this is better than kissing)
- Have a print shop make coupons she can redeem; they can be for foot rubs, back massages, a night on the town or whatever
- Have a professional photographer take your picture; then present her with an 8"x10" or 11"x 14" already

framed
- Buy her a gag gift at a comedy store (one in good taste)
- Have a "welcome" sign made for your front door with both of your names on it (put her name first)
- Whistle at her from time to time (you know, the whistle that says, "Hey, baby, you look good")
- When one of her favorite songs comes on the radio at home, find her and dance with her in whatever room you find her
- Keep a picture of her in your office (make it a large picture and put it in a prominent place)
- Call her a pet name such as honey, sweetheart or darling, as often as possible
- When she gets pregnant, go to the prep classes with her
- Make breakfast for her, and serve it to her in bed on her birthday or Mothers' Day
- Cuddle (This was the number one survey answer. Your wife just wants you to hold her, so she can feel secure and safe. If you don't want someone else holding her, then you do it)
- Agree to not fight in front of anyone (This especially includes your children. Stick to your agreement)

Do you want to know what would happen if you just did ten percent of these things? After the surveys were tabulated, I let some women read the results. Here is what they said about some of the things on this list:

"When my husband rubs my feet, I appreciate his caring so much. I want to make him feel good and cared for."

"If my husband did these kinds of things, I would knock myself out trying to please him. He would feel so good, eat so good, have every little thing our budget could squeeze into his hands. I'd make sure he felt appreciated!"

"My husband started out doing many of these things. As time went on, he stopped doing them. Then he wanted to know what was wrong with me. When he started trying to please me again, like when we were first married, he was shocked at how my attitude had changed."

"We are newlyweds. My husband does a lot of this stuff. He is a happy man and I am happy. I am going to see that he stays happy."

"After forty years of marriage you forget what it was like when you started out. I remember my husband satisfying me physically, emotionally, and sexually. I guess that's why they call them the good old days. If he would start doing some of these things again, I would see that he calls this time in our lives the good new days. He just thinks we have had our best times. Not yet, we haven't."

You can take the advice and opinions of your wife, mingle them with your own opinions and sometimes come up with some very good ideas. Your wife should be the first source you seek when confronted by a problem. If you get into this habit of soliciting your wife's counsel, you will find life much more enjoyable.

14

Enjoying Weekly Dates

Two wives compared notes about dates with their husbands. The first wife said, "Where we were, the moon was so romantic and bright, you could read a newspaper by it."

"Sounds wonderful," said the other wife expectantly. "What did your husband do?"

Replied the wife, "He read the paper."

I hope this does not sound familiar, but my survey wives tell me it is all too true. It seems once a man gets comfortable in his marriage, he starts ignoring his wife when opportune times arrive. This would have never happened before marriage, when the man was always looking for another opportunity to further his relationship with his "girl."

Places You Shouldn't Go

One thing I must do in this section is to advise you where not to go. As a rule, do not go to bars or other places that serve alcoholic beverages as their main business. More heartaches, arguments, hard feelings, divorces, injuries, deaths, and other negative afflictions start in bars than any of us would ever care to admit.

Other places not to go are where cigarette smoke is heavy, such as some bowling alleys, pool halls, etc. These are not healthy for you either.

Last of all, do not go to casinos or other gambling establishments, including Bingo halls. Arguments over money are a top cause of divorce. Losing money in gambling, even at Bingo, is a path down which you should not want to travel.

Rather than alcohol, tobacco, and gambling, please spend your money on your wife. She is a much better prize than any you will ever win in a gambling hall. Enough said.

Suggested Short, Fun Dates

Below is a list of dates you can pick from. Just keep one thing in mind as you go through these, you do not need to go on all these dates. You may only go on ten or twenty of them. You may go on forty or fifty of them. You may be an ambitious husband and try to do all the dates listed. The intent here is to provide you with a list of dates wives have suggested. Some were young wives and some were older wives. Just pick out one date for this week and do it. As you go through the list and think of other dates, write them in the columns at the side of the page and fulfill them, too.

Remember this observation from an unknown author— "There is nothing busier than the ant, yet it finds time to go to picnics." You may pick out a date that costs nothing, or a date that costs a lot. Some dates take some planning and arrangements, and some can be done on the spur of the moment. Most dates are best announced ahead of time so the anticipation builds up to the day and time of the date. Other dates are good as surprises. You decide. Just do it, and do it now.

This is a comprehensive list of fun, short, dates suggested by the hundreds of wives who responded to the questionnaire:

- Ate out
- Attend a play
- Attended the symphony
- Attend a concert

- Backpacking
- Bicycle trip
- Biking around Lake Tahoe
- Bowling
- Buy your wife some flowers
- Camping
- Candlelight dinner
- Church dinner
- Cook-out in the park
- Dancing
- Dinner on a harbor cruise
- Dinner at a live show
- Explored on back roads
- Drive to a lake
- Fed the ducks in a campground
- Family reunion
- Game night with friends
- Go hiking
- Went to lunch at a mansion
- Go boating alone
- Go sit by a lake and relax
- Go water skiing
- Go to a theme park
- Go to the opera
- Go to boat races
- Go out of town
- Got a sitter and went to a hotel
- Go to the zoo
- Have a midnight dinner
- Ice skating
- Just being together
- Horseback riding
- Make out in the car

- Midnight swims
- Miniature golf
- Movies
- Park overlooking the city
- Parking
- Picnic on a deserted beach
- Picnic in a cemetery
- Play in a park
- Play golf
- Rode around on a motorcycle
- Roller skating
- Sailing
- Scuba dive
- Shopping
- Short day trips
- Spend a night in a hotel
- Snow skiing
- Rafting
- Rent a limo
- Take a ride to the mountains
- Take a short day trip
- Take turns reading to each other
- Tubing
- Visit an art gallery
- Visit a museum
- Visited Montezuma's Castle
- Visited a wildlife park
- Walk along a beach
- Watched the sunset
- Sporting events
- Stayed in a condo
- Surprise birthday party
- Watching the sunrise

- Went to a romantic movie
- Water skiing
- Went to a music concert
- Went to the zoo
- Went to antique market
- Went snorkeling
- Went to a baseball game
- Went to a craft fair
- Went to a hockey game
- Went for a long drive
- Attended a company Christmas party
- Be Mr. and Mrs. Santa Claus at a children's hospital at Christmas
- Bumper boats and Miniature golf
- Buy your wife a box of chocolates
- Cooked shrimp over a campfire in the woods
- Dressed up and went to Halloween dance
- Driving around and looking at model homes
- Drove to a mountain overlooking the city at night
- Exchanged Valentines presents
- Football (Playing or watching it)
- Had a candlelight dinner in the bed of a pickup at a drive-in movie
- Have dinner in a secluded park with candles and the works
- He fixed a candlelight gourmet dinner with a friend as the waiter in his apartment
- Kidnap my husband and go to a motel
- Late evenings, discussions, planning the future
- Made passionate love in the forest after a picnic lunch
- Pickin' & Grinnin' parties (This is guitars, banjos, and singing)
- Put a mattress in the bed of a pickup, looked at the stars

and talked
- Rent a room at a hotel and have dinner there
- Spontaneous romantic privacy at home
- Surprised husband with hike in mountains, then candle light dinner in woods
- Walking around a lake after dinner
- Walking and talking in the mountains
- Went to a formal dance, given a nice, fun invitation beforehand
- Went to a park and overlooked scenery
- Went with my husband to meet his friends
- Went to a park, squirted each other with water guns
- Went to spring training games (baseball)
- Went flying with my pilot husband

15

Quarterly Dates

The man asked the live-in nanny and house worker, "Why are you leaving us? Haven't we always treated you like one of the family?"

She said, "Yes, and I'm getting pretty tired of it."

Quarterly dates are sometimes more expensive than weekly dates, and may take more planning and effort to accomplish, but not always so. Suggested here are dozens of fun dates and activities that take more planning, and probably cost more, than most of the dates suggested in the previous chapter. You may want to use any of the dates in chapter fourteen, "Your Weekly Dates," as a quarterly date, or vice versa.

Listed below are dozens of other fun dates and husband–wife activities.

- Flew to Oklahoma
- Flew to California
- Go for a ride in a glider plane
- Go on an ocean cruise
- Go to a bed and breakfast inn
- Go skydiving
- Hire a band for a dance party
- Phil Collins concert

- Salt Lake City, Utah
- San Diego, California
- Spend a weekend at a resort
- Sedona, Arizona
- Take a hot air balloon ride
- Take a helicopter ride
- Take your wife hunting
- Times Square
- Trip to Waco, Texas
- Trip to California
- Trip within state to another city
- Try bungee jumping
- Weekend in the mountains
- Visit a historical place
- Went to Phantom of the Opera
- Went to Catalina
- Attend a Broadway show of her choice
- Balloon Fiesta in Albuquerque, New Mexico
- Buy a billboard for a day, week, or month telling your wife you love her
- Christmas vacation in New Mexico
- Dinner in a hot air balloon over the Grand Canyon
- Fly somewhere and stay a couple of days
- Flew to California for Phantom of the Opera, had lunch at Rothchild's
- Give your wife a gift certificate to go have her hair done
- Go to a fancy dance/ball and dance all night
- Go for a ride in a small plane around your city or state
- Get a therapeutic massage from a professional masseuse or masseur
- Go to a good hotel out of town. Ask the hotel to put on their outside marquee, "Welcome, Mrs. Cronin" (use your last name)

- Go to a resort hotel for a weekend
- Going to a Neil Diamond concert
- Have an expensive romantic dinner
- Have a surprise birthday party at a McDonald's or another place she would not suspect. (An affluent friend of mine did this for his wife. Many of their friends were also wealthy and all the Mercedes, Lexus, Cadillac's and other such cars sure looked funny filling the parking lot.)
- Hire a comedian for a twenty- to thirty-minute show. Contact your local comedy club; make sure he understands the kind of jokes to tell.
- Hire a magician for a show in your home
- Hire a disc jockey for a dance party
- Hire a clown to put on a twenty to thirty minute show at a party
- Honeymoon on Catalina Island.
- Join softball, volleyball or other co-ed team sports together for the quarter
- Make a short commercial and pay a radio station to play it on your wife's favorite station. Play it at a time she will hear it. Tell her you love her in the commercial.
- Write your wife a letter telling her how much you appreciate her and all she has done for you this quarter. Be specific! Then mail it to her.
- Order a dinner catered at your house or a hotel room
- Participate in a cleanup campaign. Clean up a river, a park, a roadside, etc.
- Put up a banner in front of your house that says, "I love my wife." Put it up inside if you are too embarrassed to put it outside.
- Rent a banquet facility and invite your wife's friends. Have people say good things about her at the banquet, including a prepared speech by you telling how much

you appreciate her and love her.
- Rent a limousine for a few hours and ride around your town. You can also go to dinner, a movie, or anyplace else that comes to mind. (A friend of mine rented a limo on his wife's birthday, gathered her parents and children and then picked her up from work to go to lunch, pre-arranged with her boss. She knew he was coming to pick her up for lunch, but had no idea he would be in a limo. When the driver opened the door to let her in the back, there sat her parents and children. She will never forget.)
- Season tickets to professional basketball team
- Sign up for a college class together
- Sit in the audience of a T.V. show while it is taping
- Stay in a condo for the weekend
- Take a computer training class together
- Take a bus ride on a sightseeing tour around your state
- Take a ride to the mountains or a drive into the country
- Take a camera on a photography trip
- Take a trip on a train somewhere in your state or a neighboring state
- Take a scuba diving or snorkeling trip
- Throw your wife a party for her birthday
- Took back roads over the Rockies
- Weekend stay at a lake in a friend's trailer
- Went to a Broadway play
- Went to San Diego for two nights without kids
- Went to see David Copperfield
- Went to a Frank Sinatra concert
- Went out of town for three days
- Write a book together. It can be fiction, nonfiction, a children's book, a novel, etc. You do not have to publish it.
- Write your life history together. Your children and

grandchildren will love reading this, and they may read it soon if you try the skydiving.

16

Make Your Anniversary Dates Special

A husband and wife were sitting across the room from each other one evening when the husband said, "Life is like the universe."

Several weeks passed, and the couple was seated in their favorite chairs again in the same room. The wife asked, "Why is life like the universe?"

Several more weeks passed and the husband and wife were in their usual places. The husband said, "Okay, have it your way. Life is not like the universe."

Never Miss Celebrating Your Wedding Anniversary

Your anniversary commemoration may only be for a few hours, or it may last overnight, for the weekend, or a long weekend. It could last three or four nights at home or away from home. If you can't go out of town to celebrate, then do it at home. Lock the doors and don't answer the phone (you can unplug it!). Don't answer the door—celebrate as if you were at a hotel in another city. Have dinner in an unusual spot—a picnic on the bed, or have a candlelight and crystal dinner on the patio. Try pizza in the bathtub, with candles burning for the only light.

If you can only afford to go out for dinner, then do that. But never let your wedding anniversary go by without celebrating it in some way. An anniversary is one of the four biggest days of the year in a woman's life.

Suggested Anniversary Dates

You may not do one of these ideas every year, but try to do some of them sometime during the next several years. If your circumstances do not allow, you can substitute this chapter for the five-year trip chapter. You should do some of these, sometime, during your fifty to seventy-five years together. You can also use a weekly date or quarterly date as an anniversary date.

In my survey, I asked the respondents what they would like to do on their next anniversary. The answers are listed here. Many wives left the answer blank. Several wives put question marks in the space. All answers are not listed. Keep in mind that many wives gave the same answers. The answers that were given most frequently have an asterisk after them.

- Go to a Broadway play
- Dinner and dancing★
- Go to a resort for the weekend★
- Go to Hawaii
- Go to Astroworld all day long
- Alaska trip
- Go to San Antonio, Texas
- Have some romance
- Go away with no kids overnight★
- Go camping
- Have a romantic dinner out★
- Limo ride

- Quiet time together★
- Return to Europe
- Rent a motel room and order pizza
- Take a trip★
- Weekend at bed and breakfast★
- Take a cruise★
- Go to another town to dinner and stay overnight★
- Fly somewhere, stay in a hotel and sight-see★
- Have a catered dinner at home, complete with servers and a live string quartet
- Rent a houseboat for a long weekend on a lake
- Rent a cabin for a long weekend in the mountains★
- Rent a motor home for the weekend and see a part of your state
- Spend time on a date, anywhere, alone

17

Treat Yourselves to Five-year Trips

One woman told another, "Last year we took a trip around the world. This year we are going someplace else."

When you plan a five-year trip, it probably will take the place of your anniversary trip for the year. You will have had five years to save the money for this trip. It is super special, and probably will be more costly than a normal anniversary celebration. These trips create really great memories.

Plan your five-year trip several years before you take it, and start putting money away. Find out how much plane tickets are going to cost, hotels, car rentals or anything else that goes with the trip. Then you know how much it is going to cost and how much you have to save each week toward the trip. Allow about ten percent more for inflation and another ten percent for good measure.

When to Plan Your Trips

The time to plan your first five-year trip is on your honeymoon. Oh, all right, you were busy. Then plan it when you get home from your honeymoon. The time to plan for your twenty-five-year trip is on your twenty-year trip. Five years ago, my wife and I went on a cruise to the Caribbean for our twenty-fifth anniversary. My pocket change went into the piggy bank and an amount from each paycheck went into savings. When the day came, we got on the boat and cruised without worrying about the money. Cars, clothes, and electronic toys all wear out and get old, but the memories you create on these special dates will warm your hearts forever.

Make a Preliminary Budget

To show you how little it takes to pay for a five-year trip, look at this example. If I could show you how to go to Hawaii for 14 dollars a week would you be interested? If you want to go to Hawaii, it will cost you 800 dollars for two round trip plane tickets from Los Angeles to Hawaii. An average rental car will cost about 200 dollars, and a good hotel costs one thousand dollars for the week. You will need money for food and souvenirs and sight-seeing while you are there, so we will give you 200 dollars a day for that. Throw in one 100 dollars to cover tips for the week. The total comes to about three thousand five hundred dollars.

Set a Weekly or Monthly Savings Goal

You have five years to save the money for your five-year trip. You need to save 700 dollars a year to have three thousand five hundred dollars. You need to save 58 dollars and 30 cents a month, or 13 dollars and 57 cents a week to have your three thousand five hundred dollars for the Hawaii trip.

Can you really tell me that you cannot find between 14 and 18 dollars a week to go to Hawaii or wherever you want to go? A trip to Europe might cost you 20 dollars a week over the course of five years. There are many five-year trips that cost far less money than Hawaii and Europe, if you feel you cannot get that kind of money together.

Below is a list of places our survey answers listed as places wives wanted to go. The most expensive of these trips will cost you about 20 dollars a week, while the least expensive trips will cost about five dollars a week.

- Acapulco, Mexico
- Africa
- Anaheim, California
- Alaska
- Australia
- Bali
- Bicycle trip around the country
- Belgium
- Borneo
- Canada
- Cabo San Lucas, Mexico
- Caribbean
- Castle trip to Germany
- Catalina Island
- Chicago, Illinois
- China
- Cruise
- Disney World
- Disneyland
- Dominican Republic, Club Med
- Europe
- Fiji
- Fishing excursion to Canada
- France
- Germany
- Olympic Games
- Grand Old Opry
- Greece
- Guatemala
- Hawaii
- India
- Indiana
- Ireland
- Israel
- Italy
- Jamaica
- Japan
- Las Vegas, Nevada
- London, England
- Mexico
- Montana
- Montreal
- Nashville, Tennessee
- Nassau
- New Zealand
- New York City
- New England
- New Orleans
- Norway
- Paris
- Russia
- Scotland
- Scuba diving in Cozumel
- Sicily
- South America
- Spain
- Sweden
- Switzerland
- Tahiti

- The Bahamas
- The South Pacific
- Yosemite
- Washington, D.C.
- Houseboat trip, Lake Powell for a week
- Asia (Hong Kong, Korea, or Japan)

The ladies were not very specific when it came to answering the question of where they'd like to go. Half the respondents listed England as a place they wanted to visit. Germany was the number two vote getter. Australia/ New Zealand was a close third to Germany. Then came France, Italy, Ireland, Japan, Switzerland, Caribbean, Hawaii, Scotland, Alaska, and Canada. The rest were almost equal in votes.

The place you and your wife want to go matters most. Sit with a world map or atlas in front of you. Decide with your wife where you are going and start saving now. The anticipation from now until the time you leave will build and will add enthusiasm and happiness to your life.

18

Savor the Golden Years

I am always interested in how big things begin. You know how it is; you're young, you make some decisions . . . then swish, you're seventy. You've been a lawyer (or something else) for over fifty years and that white-haired lady by your side has eaten over 50,000 meals with you. How do such things happen?

—Thornton Wilder

Empty-nesters Need to Rekindle Their Romance

One big mistake some couples make after they have been together for twenty or forty years is to assume they have no more need to date. I agree they may not have a need to do exciting things every month, but they still need those special one-on-one times together. Many divorces come in that midlife period as the children are getting ready to leave or just after they leave the nest. Some couples say they had only been staying together because of the children. There is some truth to that, but it is not the whole truth.

At some point during marriage, most couples start devoting more time to their children and less time to each other. They grow apart because they spend more time serving their children than serving and spending time with each other.

When your children reach adulthood, it is time to turn more attention to your wife again. You have worked hard for twenty to forty years to raise your children; now it's your turn to enjoy being with each other again.

A Love Story Reconstructed from the Survey

The most impressive survey response I received was from a woman in her forties whose husband is in his sixties. They are both confined to wheelchairs. They make between 25 and 50 thousand dollars a year. She stated in her response that her husband does not need to schedule time with her because they are together every day, "and wouldn't have it any other way." For her three favorite dates she listed, "Made passionate love in the middle of a forest after a picnic lunch, Phantom of the Opera and supper out," and "just went for a long drive and talked, watched the sunset colors play on harvested fields."

When asked about three dates she would like to have, she wrote, "Make love in an airplane. We've done it everywhere else, including a motorboat going in circles in the middle of a lake without a driver." Then, "Dinner Harbor Cruise," and "Champagne dinner in a hot air balloon over the Grand Canyon."

This woman in love also stated, "My work is my life, and our life together is one long date. Our whole life is a date. We travel and volunteer, and turn every trip, journey, etc. that we take into a date. Every day is a date to us."

When I list this woman's dates, keep in mind I am talking about a household income of less than 50 thousand dollars. She ate over fifty dinners in a restaurant last year with her husband. They watched twenty movies at theaters. They went on picnics, rides in the country, fishing, and looking for animals in the forest. After they were married, they visited Massachusetts,

Nevada, Colorado, California, New Mexico, Alaska, Utah, Kansas, Washington, D.C., Texas, Florida, and Minnesota.

This couple has also had ice cream at a mall, eaten apples and had cheese and crackers while watching a sunset in the desert. Also on their list was toasting marshmallows while watching Halley's comet through a twelve-hundred-millimeter telescope, and reading books out on a lake. She says, "We say 'I love you' a minimum of twelve times a day and mean every syllable of it."

Both have disabilities, and the only time they make excuses for not going out is when they become fatigued or are in too much pain—then they stay home and rest. She also says they stayed in a hotel and called room service and had a very sensual meal in the room overlooking the night lights. He has sent her flowers six times in the last year.

The survey asked her to list her last three anniversary gifts and she wrote, "Every year we share laughter—the most important gift of all. If we see something that strikes our fancy, we get it. To show love is so important, why wait for commercially approved days: at our age time is too short to wait, especially when disabled, and our ability to 'actively' participate in sharing is less and less every year." She also lists her three favorite gifts as "laughter, joy, and hope."

Her husband opens car doors and other doors for her (while in a wheelchair). He hugs her several times a day, kisses her several times a day, holds her hand, and puts his arm around her in public. They do not sit on the couch together because of their disability. For her three happiest memories, she listed, "the day we married," and "the night we listened to wolves howl in the distance when we were on a canoe trip in the boundary waters of Minnesota. We were huddled together for warmth . . . we talked . . . then went silent to listen to nature." The last favorite memory I won't list since I am trying to keep this book in the "G" or at least "PG" rating. Let's just say it had to do with something they did on a houseboat. She said he was "mischievous and had a twinkle in his eye."

They have been to Universal Studios, Sea World, and San Diego. Tucson and Alpine, Arizona have also been on their itinerary. She wants to visit Yellowstone, Williamsburg in the fall, the Black Hills of South Dakota, Australia, New Zealand, Ireland, and Scotland. Something tells me she will. She said they like picking up rocks from streambeds, and they have a hummingbird feeder to attract the little birds they love to watch. I'm much intrigued by how their wheelchairs can negotiate rough terrain.

Too Old to Date? No Way!

All right, after reading about this woman and her husband, can you jump up and say you are too old or too disabled to date? I know there are some people in that condition, but please don't give up on yourselves.

I saw on the news a man in his eighties who had just run a marathon (twenty-six miles). He had retired at seventy-two, sat around waiting to die and when it did not happen, decided he might as well do something until it did happen. I am not suggesting you go out and run a marathon. However, I'll bet there are quite a few things listed in this book you are still able to do.

One woman wrote of her marriage of over thirty years. She and her husband are over fifty. "We have a great, fun marriage—he is the nicest person I've ever met—works too hard, but on our exploring expeditions it is laughs, fun, and romance. He spoils me rotten, and after thirty-one years I thank God for him every day."

Another woman and her husband are over seventy-one years old and have been married to each other for fifty-one years.

They have a household income of less than 25 thousand dollars a year. She wrote that they had visited all fifty states and taken cruises to Panama, Mexico and Hawaii. They also have been to Europe.

Formulate Your Own Golden-years Philosophy

Another woman who returned a survey listed her age in the fifties, with a husband in his sixties. She wrote, "After spending many years (over thirty-one) with each other—going places that cost nothing to spending lots, the thing that is most important to me is I'm still married to my best friend. We . . . keep meeting challenges each day to continue to grow and not become bored with each other. Each day of life is a gift and it is a big challenge to keep life exciting, but worth it. Listening to each other and talking to each other in consideration is of great value. Finally, look for the pluses in your relationship and not chew on the negatives, both [of you need to] grow."

You may have formed the habit of doing nothing or doing little for and with your wife. It is not too late to break that habit, whatever your age. In your mind, you may argue with yourself and imagine that it is too late. I am telling you it is not. Listen to your heart instead of your mind. The heart is a higher source of right than the mind. Now is the time for you to act!

19

Treating Your Wife Right Now

Love is not getting old, but giving, not a wild dream of pleasure, and madness of desire . . . oh, no, love is not that — it is goodness and honor, and peace and pure living, yes, love is that; and it is the best thing in the world, and the thing that lives the longest.

—Henry Van Dyke

He Should've and He Did

Judi Villa, a newspaper reporter for the Phoenix Gazette, told me that her husband surprised her once on a date. He told her he had to go to the store and would be right back. They had already dressed for their date. About five minutes later she heard a knock on the front door and she answered it. Her husband was standing there and held out a single red rose and told her he was there to pick up his date. She felt like a princess. How do you think your wife would feel if you did this? What do you think the end result would be after dinner? That is the essence of treating your wife right now. Once he thought of how he "Could've," he "Should've," and he did.

The opposite of this is you "could've," but an excuse enters your mind. At that point, you fail to act, in which case, the

163

scenario becomes, "should've," and didn't. Judi's husband knows the difference in having a date and having a romantic date.

Give Thought to What *Right* Is

To treat your wife right requires you to give some thought to what right is. When you think of the word right, several concepts come to the mind. Definitions like fair, equitable, proper, justice, rectitude and others sound fine when describing the word. But you need to transcend the simple definitions. Instead of words flowing through your mind, try images. A picture is worth a thousand words.

Picture images that bring happiness, joy, warmth and a smile to your face. Think back to your wedding day. Close your eyes. Remember the happiness in your wife's eyes and the smile on her face? Remember those present and the excited chatter of the occasion? Remember your feelings? These images bring joy.

Now come back closer to the present. Recall a happy time with your wife that you recently experienced. If you have to, close your eyes again. Once you have that image in your mind, focus on how you felt. Now, focus on her. How did she feel? Remember her smile? Images are much more powerful than words. Why wouldn't anyone want to have thousands of those images?

Your Life Is the Sum of Your Memories

Man is that he might have joy. The way to have joy is to have as many happy images stored away as you can fit into the storage modules of your brain and call them to your awareness often.

Your life is the sum of your memories. The only way to have those memories is to live them. The only way to live them is to dream them first. Once you have an image in your mind of what can be, you can make it so. According to Walt Disney, "If you can dream it, you can do it."

In our case, I am not talking about creating Disneyland. I am talking about making wherever you are with your wife the happiest place on earth for yourselves. If you happen to be at Disneyland—so much the better. I am talking about creating little pieces of your life, as you would like to see them happen. Create happiness. Treating your wife right now opens the door to happier times for both of you and for your entire family.

Dream Your Future into Reality

It was not that difficult for Disney to create Disneyland in his mind. It was a dream. To create Disneyland in reality was a bit more difficult, but he did it. The first step is a choice to create dreams. They may even be daydreams of what you would like to have happen in your life. You create all things in your mind before they exist physically. Creation without thought is impossible.

The difficulty lies in taking action to bring your dreams to reality. Imagine a construction crew arriving on the scene of a vacant lot and the supervisor climbing out of his truck and saying, "Go to work, men." The men stand there and look at him, and finally one brave soul says, "What should we build?" The supervisor replies, "I don't know, nobody thought of it yet, but get to work." No blueprints, no instruction, no direction, just go aimlessly to work. Have you given any thought to your dating habits with your wife? Do you have blueprints on how to create good dating experiences?

This book contains blueprints and instructions on how to date. Use these instructions for creating a more-satisfying relationship with your wife. Create the relationship you have already dreamed.

The chapters in this book are the mental blueprints to help you physically create some kind of date. Action is still needed. Treating your wife right requires adding adornment to the creation.

Use Adornment in Your Dating Life

A man can build a house with footings, a foundation, walls, and a roof. He can put insulation in the walls and attic, shingles on the roof, drywall on the ceiling and supporting studs, and then he can tape and texture the drywall and paint it. Then he can add sinks, toilets, towel and toilet paper holders, tubs, showers, light fixtures, electrical sockets, light switches, windows, shelves in closets, doors, and door knobs. When done, he has used dozens of yards of concrete, scores of studs, and hundreds of feet of wire and pipe. He has even put tile and carpet on that perfectly good concrete floor to cover it.

Then he moves into the house with a wife. The adornment process has just begun. There are curtains to buy, and curtains do not hang right without curtain rods. There has to be a carpet to cover the toilet lid, mini-blinds over the windows and curtains. The beds need blankets and bedspreads, too. On top of the spreads, there have to be pillows to make them look nice. Knick-knacks hang all over the kitchen walls, and you need paper towel holders under the cabinets and a few dozen magnets on the refrigerator. Paintings go in the living room. Family pictures line the entryway into the house. A clock in every room is a necessity. A mirror or two hung in various rooms reflect the plants, real or silk.

I could go on, of course, but the point is, women like things adorned. Dates are no different. A date is a date. However, an adorned date is something to remember. The opening paragraph of this chapter is an example of an adorned date. Judi's husband adorned it with a flower. More important than that, when Judi said she was ready to go he didn't just get up out of the recliner and give her the flower. He was waiting at the front door after ringing the doorbell, ready to pick up his date. Judi's husband took that extra step to ensure a lasting impression. Judi can live to be a hundred and fifty and she will always have that image in her mind and the warm feelings that went with it.

It will take another book to write of all the ways a man could adorn his dates. Teenagers are the best at this adornment process. When my daughter Jacey was dating I saw young men show up at the house with flowers and cards for no reason. They left notes on her car, and they asked permission to leave notes on her bedroom door or in her bedroom. They also filled her bedroom with balloons and told her that inside one of the balloons was a message; she had to pop them all to find the message. These young men also brought by a group of balloons with a message on them. They brought her posters with all kinds of designs and attached messages. Young men also mailed very special letters to her.

When I was dating my wife, she claims I used to stop by her house in the early morning hours on my way to work and put poems under her car windshield wipers. I have no recollection of acting like that. But, she has the poems and other letters she says I wrote (the handwriting does suspiciously look a lot like mine).

Treating your wife right now entails the adornment process on occasion. You should not adorn every date. However, you should adorn some dates to create those special memories that last a lifetime. I could ask Judy where she went to eat with her husband last September and she may not remember. I'll bet Judy remembers where she ate the night her husband rang the doorbell and picked up his date. Whether it was Taco Bell or an expensive steak house, it didn't matter. Judy's husband had already made the date a memorable one.

Do It Right Now

The other part of the title to this chapter exceeds the word "right." That word is "now." You can treat your wife right, but if you do not treat her right "now," you are missing an opportunity. Now requires action today, this hour, this minute, maybe this second.

DO IT NOW is the key phrase. In communication, we need not only to be clear about what it is we want to happen, we need to be clear about when we want it to happen.

One day, I was on the phone in another room away from my wife and suddenly needed a pen. I called to her from the other room and said, "Honey, can you bring me a pen?" She couldn't see me and did not know I was on the phone. She yelled back, "Sure honey, I'll get it." I waited. No pen. I couldn't see my wife doing dishes in the kitchen. Then I called to her using a louder voice, "Are you bringing me the pen?" She yelled back, "In a minute." When I called back, "I am on the phone. I NEED IT NOW," she finally understood.

Misunderstandings between husbands and wives similar to this one occur often in married households across the country every day. The result quite often is an argument. My wife did not understand that I was on the phone. I did not understand she was washing dishes. She did not know I needed the pen right then. I did not understand she was not bringing it that very minute. She did not understand that my phone conversation was too important to get up and get the pen myself. I did not understand that dishes are just as important as my phone conversation, and I should have gone and retrieved the pen myself. This could be a point of lifetime misunderstanding between husbands and wives.

Make Self-sufficiency Part of Your Basic Conduct

It boils down to making a simple plan. We will call the plan self-sufficiency. If you can help yourself, then do help yourself. If your legs are not broken, then you can get the pen. If paralysis does not grip you from the waist down, get the soda yourself. If you can bend over, pick up your own socks.

I am not saying to do this every time. But do these things more often than you are currently doing them. Give your wife a break sometimes. Help her. Then she will be glad to help you sometimes.

The truth usually is the cruelest teacher. The way to treat your wife right is to do for her all that you can. Do it now.

20

How to Serve Your Wife

The tired rich businessman came home from a hard day at the office. Then his wife announced that their cook had just quit.

"Why did she quit? I thought she was getting along quite well here."

The wife said, "She quit because of the way you talked to her on the phone this morning and insulted her."

The businessman replied, "It was a mistake. I'm really sorry. I thought I was talking to you."

If Your Wife Is a Nag, You're Probably the Reason

Some men treat their wives as hired help or worse. Rather than expecting service, they should provide it. Service and kindness are contagious. I have seen this on hundreds of occasions in my home and other homes. I have seen it in my work.

When you give a little of yourself to others, they typically return the favor. They gain a taste of the joy that service gives, and they become givers, too. When you give service, you will feel the happiness that giving brings. Giving service will convince you of its value.

When I hear a male describe his wife as a "nag," I am concerned. Why does she nag him if there is no cause? If he corrects the cause, he will be happier. Is he not man enough to admit faults and correct them?

Apply the Truly Golden Rule

If I hear a male speak of discord running rampant in his home, I can look to the male as a major part of the problem. I fully realize that a man controls no human but himself. However, there won't be such discord if the male is practicing the rule recognized by all of humanity as the most basic: "Do unto others as you would have them do unto you." Some think that this is largely a Christian philosophy. It is. However, the golden rule shows up in all the major religions and countries of the world. Where there is no religion, it is still a basic principle of law, etiquette and basic living. For instance:

- Do good, and care not to whom. (Italian)
- Do well, and dread no shame. (Scottish)
- Do what you should and let the people talk. (German)
- When it is proper, then do it. (Indian/Far East)
- Ill doers are ill deemers. (English)
- If you give no help to others you are wasting those prayers to Buddha. (Chinese)

Replacing the golden rule with anything else would be foolish. It works, and has done so for centuries, including those before the time of Christ. However, let me suggest the following rules of manhood to be used in conjunction with the golden rule. Being a man is a far higher calling than the random chance of being male. You don't have to agree with the following but think about what the phrases say about a real man and about selfish and uncultured males:

- A man is persuasive; a male bullies.
- A man is longsuffering; a male is impatient.
- A man is gentle; a male is harsh.
- A man is meek; a male is domineering.

- A man loves; a male is hurtful.
- A man is kind; a male is cruel.
- A man is knowledgeable; a male is ignorant.
- A man is sincere; a male is a hypocrite.
- A man is truthful; a male is dishonest.
- A man is faithful; a male is traitorous.
- A man is charitable; a male is selfish.
- A man is virtuous; a male is promiscuous.
- A man is confident; a male is insecure.
- A man is righteous; a male is unprincipled.
- A man serves others; a male serves only himself.

If these maxims come across as a bit harsh, I certainly do not intend them to be. The innocent are calm and thoughtful of words and events. According to the dictionary, a male is "a person of the male sex; of or pertaining to the sex that begets young by fertilizing the female; masculine." That is about it for the definition of male. Simply, a male is a person who can perform the sex act. A malefactor is a person who violates the law. Malefic is productive of evil, evil doing.

The definition of a man is, "an individual . . . at the highest level of . . . development, characterized by a highly developed brain and the ability to reason abstractly and form articulate speech." "A human . . . Manly character, courage."

What are the man-based words? There is *Mana*: a generalized, supernatural force or power, which may be concentrated in objects or persons. *Manage*: to bring about, succeed in accomplishing. *Manas*: the rational faculty of the mind. *Mandala*: a schematized representation of the cosmos, chiefly characterized by a concentric organization of geometric shapes, each of which contains an image of a deity or an attribute of deity. Between the two choices, I would rather be a man than a male.

Suggestions for How to Serve Your Wife Right

I offer the following short list of little things you can do to "serve" your wife "right," and some of them you can do right "now." Do not be afraid to get up out of your recliner and do one of them now. You are at the end of the chapter anyway—it's a good breaking point.

- Wash or wax her car
- Vacuum the carpet
- Clean out a desk or drawer
- Sweep the floor
- Clean out from under the bed
- Make the bed
- Put some dishes away
- Dust the ceiling fans
- Take out the garbage
- Dust some shelves
- Vacuum her car or your car
- Do some ironing
- Wash the dishes or dry them
- Clean out a closet
- Do the grocery shopping
- Clean the bathroom
- Fold some clothes and put them away
- Help clear the table of dishes after a meal
- Cook breakfast, lunch, or dinner
- Pick up some clothes from the cleaners
- Put away the condiments, etc., after a meal
- Pick up the kids, or deliver the kids where they need to go
- Change the air conditioning or heating unit filters
- Clean out the garage or clean up the carport

- Take your wife by the arm, sit her down, and bring her a cool drink
- Clean out the refrigerator or defrost the freezer
- Put a load of clothes in the washing machine or dryer
- Pick up some clothes that are lying around, especially if they are yours

21

Nice Things To Say to Your Wife

Young man at a college football game: "Look at that guy run. He'll be our best man before the season is over."

Young woman: "Oh darling, what a wonderful way to propose."

Hearing More Than Just Words

Following our theme of creating dominant thoughts and habits, this chapter suggests how you should talk to your wife. Communication, and speech itself, consists of much more than words. It involves tone, inflection, pronunciation, volume, and body language. As discussed in a previous chapter, the art of communication involves all the senses, and sound is only one of them. When you speak, the woman hearing you does not just hear the words, she hears what is behind your words, too.

The list of suggested things to say to your wife that follows in this chapter was easy to create. Getting you to say them in the right way may be more difficult. When you were a teenager, you had a parent or other adult that used a certain sentence that all adults use universally. That sentence is "Don't you use that tone of voice with me." You recognize that sentence, don't you?

177

You can say "Right!" with animated enthusiasm, and it means total agreement. Or you can say with a sneer, "Right," and it means total disagreement. Same word—but the tone and expression give opposite meanings. The tone of voice you want to use with your wife is one with caring, understanding, tenderness, compassion, empathy, and love. If you violate this tone, it matters not what the words are that you speak. The wrong tone of voice will convey inconsiderate, cold hearted, unkind, and possibly even cruel or vicious meaning to your words.

I want to make you aware of a habit that some men develop over the years: poor tone of voice. The next time you talk to your wife, listen to your tone of voice. Especially be aware of your tone when responding to your wife.

Try This Thought-provoking Role Play

When your wife says, "Honey, can you take out the trash?" You may respond with many different tones in saying "yes." The response of, "Sure, I'll take out the trash," can have many different meanings, depending on the tone you use.

We are going to go to acting class in the next few sentences. Pretend you are reading for a part in a movie. Whoever is chosen is going to get $7 million to play the husband in this movie. I am the director of the movie. The scene is a simple one. The script can take several directions, and I, as the director, am not sure which way I am going to shoot the scene in this film. I am going to have you read one line. It is, "Sure, I'll take out the trash."

This exercise is performed while speaking aloud. However, if you are in your office at work or on a crowded bus or subway going home from work, you might want to do this exercise in your mind. Do it with passion, as though $7 million is riding on your performance to get the part for this movie.

The scene is this: you just arrived home from work two seconds ago. Your wife is in the kitchen cooking fried chicken for dinner with all the trimmings. The smell is pleasant; you like fried chicken. You have just set down the items you carried home from work on the living room couch. Your wife calls out to you from the kitchen, "Honey, can you take out the trash?" Now, I want you to repeat your line in the following ways.

Scene #1. You're tired and beat from a long day at work. Exhausted and "wiped out," you are just barely dragging your body along. Now, say your line as if you are really dejected and tired, with sagging shoulders. "Sure, I'll take out the trash."

Scene #2. You had a fight with your wife last night and have not made up. You feel she is too demanding of you. She does not express appreciation for your hard work. Say your line using your most resentful voice. "Sure, I'll take out the trash."

Scene #3. It's a pleasant spring day out. The birds are singing. Your boss just informed you that you are getting a twenty per-cent raise, a ten thousand dollar bonus, a promotion, a company car, and an expense account. You've come home with happy news, and nothing could disappoint you. All is right with the world. You made love to your wife last night. You smell your favorite dinner cooking. Now say your line lovingly. "Sure, I'll take out the trash." (Great scene, huh?)

Be Aware of Your Tone of Voice and Body Language

You have probably used these tones and several others. You could have a helping tone, a sarcastic tone, a hateful tone, an indifferent tone and myriad others. Your emotion gives the response of, "Sure, I'll take out the trash" different meanings. Be aware of the tone in which you are responding when you respond to all of her communications. A smile can be heard even when it isn't seen. Use the correct tone of voice and do as Dennis R. Deaton says, "Bestow verbal paychecks on one another."

Great Lines for Your Personal Soap Opera

The next few pages contain your lines for your personal soap opera. I hope they bring pleasantness to your life and home.

- I love you.
- Let me rub your feet.
- Let's watch the sunset tonight.
- Princess.
- How was your day?
- Can we cuddle?
- This dinner is delicious.
- What else happened?
- I love your hair.
- Hey, beautiful!
- Thank you for ironing my shirt.
- You are so sweet!
- Want to go out to dinner?
- You are beautiful.
- Let me give you a hug.
- I made the bed.
- You have the most beautiful eyes.
- You are a sweetheart.
- How do you feel?
- Want to take a walk?
- I have tickets to the concert.
- I fixed dinner.
- Let's go get an ice cream cone.
- I understand.
- Want to take a drive?
- Want to take a nap?
- Let's go dancing.
- You are so helpful.
- I filled your car with gas.
- I washed your car.

- Tell me more about it.
- I appreciate you.
- I missed you while I was gone.
- I care about you.
- I ran your bath water.
- You are pretty.
- You have the softest skin.
- You are so kind.
- Can I hold your hand?
- I cherish you.
- You are a wonderful wife.
- My darling.
- I called the baby-sitter.
- How can I help you?
- You are good to me.
- You are my Queen!
- I had your car washed.
- Thank you.
- Your hands are always so soft.
- Please.
- Can I vacuum the carpet for you?
- May I dry the dishes for/with you?
- How is that book you are reading?
- What can I do to help you get ready?
- I changed that light bulb that burned out.
- Is there something I can get for you now?
- You are a great mother to our children.
- Can we have lunch together tomorrow?
- I have some extra time tomorrow.
- Can I get something from the store for you?
- Do you want to go shopping with me?
- You do a great job keeping our house clean.
- Would you like to talk about it? I'll listen.

- I washed the dishes while you were grocery shopping.
- I am a fortunate man to have you as my wife.
- I have reservations at a cabin in the mountains.
- Let's pick up some chicken and go on a picnic.
- Is there something that needs to be fixed around here?
- Is there anything I can get for you while I am up?
- Can I get anything for you while I am at the store?
- What would you like to do for our Friday night date?
- We have reservations Friday night at your favorite restaurant.
- We have reservations next weekend at a hotel.
- Should I pick up a video for tonight while the kids are gone?
- Can I make reservations for next month at a resort?
- Let me kiss the most beautiful woman in the world.
- The movie you wanted to see is at the theater; let's go see it Saturday.
- I have tickets for this weekend to the play you wanted to see.
- I left some extra money for you to buy that dress you wanted.
- I just happen to have a thirty-dollar gift certificate for you.
- I'm taking the kids out for a couple of hours Saturday so you can have some time alone.

22

How To Use This Book

Suggested Use Number One

You may start using the information in this book immediately. All you have to do is go to the Creating Habits section and use the first of the fifty-two ideas. Read idea number one and the commentary below it. Find your wife or call her from wherever you are and schedule the first of your fifteen-minute sessions with her. Continue through the fifty-two ideas, using one each day or week. When you have completed the ideas, you have established a solid dating habit that will have improved your relationship with your wife.

After you have made the first date, you have an entire week to calculate how to achieve idea number two. I caution you: don't try to progress too fast or attempt too many ideas at once. You will start leaving some goals unfinished. As a result, you won't create the habits that will ingrain in you a solid foundation.

Suggested Use Number Two

Here is a suggestion if you don't have time to read. Go to the "Daily Dates" chapter and pick out one thing you would like to do today and then accomplish it. Also, turn to the "Nice Things to Say to Your Wife" chapter and choose something special to say to your wife today and when you see her, express it. Then pick something out of the "Weekly Dates" chapter and arrange for that fun time as well. You may choose from the chapters and select what you would like to accomplish from each chapter that applies to your situation. Each day or week you can repeat this process.

While you have the book in your hand, look at the "Quarterly Date" chapter and decide which date to go on three months from now. Arrange for that date now. An important step is to suggest the date to your wife, and if she agrees, get it scheduled. Anticipation is the enhancement that makes the date exciting.

Anticipation makes life worth living. Your wife will think about the date coming up during the entire week. She will have three months to think about that quarterly date. That gives her three months to tell her friends about her upcoming, very special time she'll be spending with you. This is an important part of dating for her—it gives her a chance to show her friends that she has a great husband. It also gives her a great deal of self-worth, knowing that you care enough to schedule weekly and quarterly dates in advance. Once these dates are scheduled, be sure to keep them and enjoy some wonderful times together.

Don't make the same mistakes you did twenty years ago. Schedule your weekly, quarterly, and anniversary dates and five-year trips. You should schedule an anniversary date one year in advance and a five-year trip five years in advance.

As you go through the ideas shared in this book, write down some more of your own. Listen to your wife. She may tell you about something she would like to do, or mention some place she would like to go. If it is a weekly date idea, you may want to write it down in the weekly dates chapter. If it is a quarterly date, you may want to write it down in the "Quarterly Dates" chapter, etc.

Suggested Use Number Three

A wise way for you to get your wife involved is to show her the book during one of your fifteen-minute talking sessions. Open to the weekly date chapter and ask your wife to go through the ideas listed there. Have her use a pen to put an X beside the things she would like to do in the left column. Do the same with the quarterly date section, anniversary section and five-year trip section.

Ask your wife to write notes in the back of the book, listing things she would like to do. She may also want to write these notes in the side columns in the chapter she is reading or in another appropriate chapter. Once she has recorded her ideas, you can put a red X beside the dates and ideas you complete in the right column. This allows you to keep track of the things you have done on your dates that she chose.

After she puts her X beside the things she would like to do, ask her to rank the ideas as much as possible, especially the five-year trips. You need to know which ideas are most important to her so you can act on them. Perhaps she would like to go to Hawaii in five years and British Columbia for a cruise five years after that. You will know which trip you are working toward. She may change her mind later, but that is all right; at least you started with a plan.

The ideas she writes down are going to be more important because those are the ideas she would really like to complete. This book is for the two of you, not just for you. This book is not all-inclusive; your wife may want to do something that is not on my lists.

You may also want to write the calendar date instead of an X beside each listing you have accomplished. This allows you to know how long it has been since you last tried an idea. The recording of month, day, and year beside the "dates" you have tried can come in handy. Recording these dates will help if you try to write in a journal or try to write your life history later. You will have all the special dates recorded in your "date" book.

Suggested Use Number Four

You may also decide to read this book. That only involves opening to the title page and starting to read. I felt it was important, in the opening chapters, to help you understand certain principles on which I try to shed more light.

More important than anything else is the actual use of the book. If you don't use it regularly, it will do you no good. Please put this book in a prominent and conspicuous place in your home or office. This will help remind you to look inside and see how you are fulfilling your goals. It will also help you decide what to do next. I will make a prediction: If you don't put the book in a conspicuous and prominent place, you will probably fail to follow its ideas and principles.

Seeing this book regularly will help create new thought patterns that will move you to action. Having this book handy will give you ideas for what you are going to do next. Until dating is again a habit, let this book be your conscience. "Out of sight, out of mind" is a true statement. Please keep this book in view so you can remember to use it.

Keeping this book in plain sight may also prod other husbands into action. If a friend, neighbor or relative sees the book on your coffee table at home, he may ask about it. Then you can convert him to the idea of dating his wife with more enthusiasm, love and ardor.

Over sixty percent of the women who answered my questionnaire stated their husbands don't schedule time to be with them. Interestingly, the divorce statistics are about the same. Do you think there is any correlation?

Review the book at least once a day to start. Later, you may want to review it once a week or once each month after you have started establishing the habit of always thinking of your wife. The constant review of its principles will help keep you on track to constant and frequent dating.

I hope you can make thinking about your wife and treating her with respect, love, compassion, patience, and loyalty a vogue thing to do in our society. May you use this book in good health for many years. And may you reap increased happiness and joy from applying many of the ideas suggested in it. You have my best wishes for increased personal success in your marriage!

Appendix

Dating Questionnaire

1. Circle your age group.

   20-30   31-40   41-50   51-60   61-70   71+

2. Circle husband's age group.

   20-30   31-40   41-50   51-60   61-70   71+

3. Years married to current husband:

   0-10   11-20   21-30   31-40   41-50   51+

4. Which marriage is this for you?

   First   Second   Third   Fourth   Fifth+

5. Which marriage for husband?

   First   Second   Third   Fourth   Fifth+

6. How many children live in your house now?

   1   2   3   4   5   6   7   8+

7. How many children have moved out?

   1   2   3   4   5   6   7   8+

8. Number of dates a year you have with your husband?

   0-10   11-20   21-30   31-40   41-50   50+

9. What is your annual household income?

   $0-25,000 $25,001-50,000 $50,001-75,000

   $75,001-100,000 $100,001-125,000

   $125,001-150,000 $150,001+

10. Number of dinners alone with your husband at your house in the last 52 weeks?

    0-10   11-20   21-30   31-40   41-50   50+

11. Number of dinners alone with your husband at a restaurant in the last 52 weeks?

    0-10   11-20   21-30   31-40   41-50   50+

12. How much was the average bill for the two of you to eat dinner out?

    $_____

13. How many times did you have lunch alone with your husband in the last 52 Weeks?

    0-10   11-20   21-30   31-40   41-50   50+

14. How much was the average bill for the two of you to eat lunch?

    $_____

15. Number of movies you and your husband attended in the last 52 weeks? _____

16. Number of movies rented and viewed with your husband in the last 52 weeks? _____

17. Number of times you were alone with your husband at a hotel in the last 52 weeks? _____

18. How many nights did the two of you spend alone at the motel/hotel? _____

19. How much was the average bill per night for the motel/hotel? $_____

20. What is your husband's occupation?

_____

21. What is your occupation? (Housewife is an occupation.)

_____

22. List the ages of the children living with you now.

_____

23. Do you take walks with your husband?

    Yes   No

24. Does your husband schedule time to be alone with you each week?

    Yes   No

25. List three things you would like to do on a date that you have not yet done.

(1)_____

(2)_____

(3)_____

26. List what you did on your three most favorite dates since you have been married.

(1)_____

(2)_____

(3)_____

27. List what you did on your three most favorite dates prior to being married.

(1)_____

(2)_____

(3)_____

28. In the last 52 weeks, how many Sabbaths did you attend church?

None   1-10   11-20   21-30   31-40   41-52

29. In the last 52 weeks, how many Sabbaths did your husband attend church?

None   1-10   11-20   21-30   31-40   41-52

30. How many trips have you taken with your husband on a commercial airline? _____

31. List the foreign countries you have visited since you have been married. Use one line for each trip. (Example: 1. Germany, France, Austria. 2. Mexico)

(1)_____

(2)_____

Please list any other trips/countries visited on the last page of this questionnaire.

32. List the states in America you have visited since you have been married. Use one line for each trip, as in question #31.

(1)_____

(2)_____

(3)_____

Please list any other trips/states visited on the last page of this questionnaire.

33. List any ship cruises you have taken, listing places visited.

(1)_____

(2)_____

(3)_____

34. List four dates you enjoyed having with your husband that cost no money.

(1)_____

(2)_____

(3)_____

(4)_____

35. List the three most expensive dates you've shared with your husband. List approximate cost; i.e., trip to England, $5,600. This can be trips abroad, your honeymoon, etc.

(1)_____

(2)_____

(3)_____

36. List five dates you have enjoyed going on with your husband that cost $1 to $20.

(1)_____

(2)_____

(3)_____

(4)_____

(5)_____

37. What kind of structure do you live in?

Apartment   House   Town-house   Condo

Other_____

38. What was the purchase price of the house you are living in now?

Under $10,000 $10,000-50,000 $50,001-100,000
$100,001-150,000 $150,001-200,000 $200,001-250,000
$250,001-300,000   over $300,000

39. What is the monthly payment on your house, condo, town house or apartment? $_____

40. What excuses does your husband give for not going out on dates?

(1)_____

(2)_____

(3)_____

41. What excuses do you give for not going out on dates?

(1)_____

(2)_____

(3)_____

42. List three dates you have taken with your husband that cost $20 to $50.

(1)_____

(2)_____

(3)_____

43. Circle the total amount you spend on car payment(s) each month.

None $1-$100 $101-200 $201-300

$301-400 $401-500 $501-600 $601+

44. Number of times your husband gave you flowers in the last 52 weeks?

None   1   2   3   4   5   6   7   8   9

10   11   12   13+

45. Number of boxes of chocolates your husband gave you in the last 52 weeks?

None   1   2   3   4   5   6   7   8   9

10   11   12   13+

46. List other gifts your husband gave you in the last 52 weeks, not counting Christmas, your anniversary, your birthday or Mothers' Day.

(1)_____

(2)_____

(3)_____

47. List the gift and approximate cost of your last three anniversary gifts.

(1)_____

(2)_____

(3)_____

48. List three favorite gifts you have received from your husband for Mothers' Day.

(1)_____

(2)_____

(3)_____

49. List your three favorite gifts your husband gave you for your birthday.

(1)_____

(2)_____

(3)_____

50. Does your husband open the car door for you when you enter/exit the car?

    Never   Occasionally   Usually   Always

51. Would you like for him to open the car door for you?

    Yes   No

52. Does your husband hold open doors for you when you go places like restaurants or movies?

    Never   Occasionally   Usually   Always

53. Would you like for him to hold open doors for you?

    Yes   No

54. Do you hold hands in public when you go out?

    Never   Occasionally   Usually   Always

55. Would you like for him to hold hands with you in public?

    Yes   No

56. Does your husband kiss you in public?

    Yes   No

57. Would you like for your husband to kiss you in public?

    Yes   No

58. Does your husband put his arm around your shoulders/waist in public?

    Yes   No

59. Would you like your husband to put his arms around you in public?

    Yes   No

60. Does your husband call you from work to express love or check on you?

        Never   Occasionally   Most days   Every day

61. Do you like it when he calls to check on you?

Yes   No

62. How many times a day does your husband tell you he loves you?

    . Never   1   2   3   4   5   6   7   8   9   10   11+

63. Do you like it when he tells you he loves you?

Yes   No

64. How many times a day does your husband hug you?

        Never   1   2   3   4   5   6   7   8   9   10   11+

65. Do you like it when he hugs you?

    Yes   No

66. How many times a day does your husband kiss you?

        Never   1   2   3   4   5   6   7   8   9   10   11+

67. Do you like it when he kisses you?

    Yes   No

68. When you are at home, do you sit on the couch together or in separate chairs?

        Together   Separate

69. Would you like for him to sit with you on the couch?

     Yes   No

70. List your three happiest memories with your husband.

(1)_____

(2)_____

(3)_____

71. What would you like to do on your next anniversary?

_____

72. What percentage of your household income goes to run the household?

     Less than 50; 51-60; 61-70; 71-80; 81-90; 91-100

73. What is the average amount your husband spends on himself each month? $_____

74. What is the average amount your husband spends on you each month? $_____

75. What does your husband do alone now that you wish he would do with you? (golf, fish, hunt, exercise, etc.)

_____

76. How much money do you put into savings accounts each month? $_____

77. How many savings accounts do you have?

     1   2   3   4   5   6+

78. List four dates you enjoyed that cost $51 to $100.

(1)_____

(2)_____

(3)_____

(4)_____

79. List three dates you enjoyed that cost $101-$500.

(1)_____

(2)_____

(3)_____

80. Number of times a year you and your husband spend the weekend alone away from home?

    Never   1   2   3   4   5   6   7   8   9

    10   11   12   13+

81. If you attend church, which denomination?

_____

82. List four dates you would like to take with your husband that cost no money.

(1)_____

(2)_____

(3)_____

(4)_____

83. What three places in the United States would you like to visit?

(1)_____

(2)_____

(3)_____

84. What three places in the world other than the United States would you like to visit?

(1)_____

(2)_____

(3)_____

85. Would you like to take a trip on a train to visit a place in the United States?

    Yes   No

86. Would you like to take a trip on a bus to visit a place in the United States?

Yes   No

87. Would you like to take a trip on a plane to visit a place in the United States?

Yes   No

88. Where in your state would you like to visit in the next year?

(1)_____

(2)_____

(3)_____

89. Where in your state would you like to visit in the next five years?

(1)_____

(2)_____

(3)_____

90. Date-wise, what three things is your husband doing now that you would like to see him keep doing?

(1)_____

(2)_____

(3)_____

91. Date-wise, what three things is your husband not now doing that you would like to see him do?

(1)_____

(2)_____

(3)_____

92. Date-wise, what three things is your husband now doing that you would like to have him stop doing?

(1)_____

(2)_____

(3)_____

93. Is your husband your best friend?

Yes   No

94. What would you like to do each week with your husband that you are not now doing?

_____

_____

_____

95. What can your husband do to help you prepare for dates?

_____

_____

_____

96. Would you trade baby-sitting duties with friends, relatives and neighbors to free up time to spend with your husband and so that they can spend time with their husbands?

Yes   No

97. Would you like to have a date a week with your husband?

Yes   No

98. Is there room for improvement in dating habits with your husband?

Yes   No

Index

About the Author

Stan Cronin was born in Barnwell, South Carolina, and raised in Arizona. His wife, Jereyne Archer DeRohwer, was born in Burbank, California. They married more than three decades ago and now live in the Phoenix, Arizona metropolitan area. They are the parents of three children: Jacey, Jared, and Jenny. To date, they have been blessed with three grandchildren: Logan, Carlee and Landen.

Stan was a police officer for the Phoenix Police Department for over twenty years, from the mid-1970s to the mid-1990s.

His observations of thousands of family fights during his career caused him to recognize the three possible outcomes for marriages: failed, managing to make-do, and cheerfully successful.

Seeing failed marriages fueled his desire to discover what "successfully" married couples do to keep the passion alive. He interviewed scores of wives and distributed over one thousand surveys to married women in ten states to get the information for this book. These wives were forthright about what was taking place inside their homes. This book is the result of those interviews. The ideas presented here are not just those of the author, but are primarily those of the wives.

The author wants all who will, to have at their fingertips some of the "secrets" that create a happy, peaceful and long lasting marriage, and he truly hopes that this book will bring much happiness to many.